your active child

HOW TO BOOST PHYSICAL, EMOTIONAL, AND COGNITIVE DEVELOPMENT THROUGH AGE-APPROPRIATE ACTIVITY

rae pica

Contemporary Books

Chicago   New York   San Francisco   Lisbon   London   Madrid   Mexico City
Milan   New Delhi   San Juan   Seoul   Singapore   Sydney   Toronto

Library of Congress Cataloging-in-Publication Data

Pica, Rae, 1953–
    Your active child : how to boost physical, emotional, and cognitive development through age-appropriate activity / Rae Pica.
        p.   cm.
    Includes bibliographical references.
    ISBN 0-07-140558-5
    1. Physical fitness for children.   2. Movement education.   3. Children—Health and hygiene.   4. Cognitive learning.   I. Title.

GV443.P49   2003
613.7'043—dc21
        2002041492

This book is dedicated to all those who work tirelessly to ensure that movement and play are part of children's lives and education.

pp. 156-157: PE evaluation checklist reprinted from "It's Time for Your School's Physical Education Checkup: How Are You Doing?" with permission of the National Association for Sport and Physical Education (NASPE), 1900 Association Drive, Reston, VA 20191, USA.

pp. 212-213: "Active Start: A Statement of Physical Activity Guidelines for Children Birth to Five Years" reprinted with permission of the National Association for Sport and Physical Education (NASPE), 1900 Association Drive, Reston, VA 20191, USA.

pp. 215-221: "IPA Declaration of the Child's Right to Play" reprinted with permission of the American Association for the Child's Right to Play (IPA/USA).

pp. 224-228: "Choosing the Right Sport or Physical Activity Program for Your Child" reprinted with permission of the National Association for Sport and Physical Education (NASPE), 1900 Association Drive, Reston, VA 20191, USA.

1 2 3 4 5 6 7 8 9 0   AGM/AGM   2 1 0 9 8 7 6 5 4 3

ISBN 0-07-140558-5

McGraw-Hill books are available at special quantity discounts to use as premiums and sales promotions, or for use in corporate training programs. For more information, please write to the Director of Special Sales, Professional Publishing, McGraw-Hill, Two Penn Plaza, New York, NY 10121-2298. Or contact your local bookstore.

This book is printed on acid-free paper.

Contents

Part I: What You Need to Know

Part II: What You Need to Do

Acknowledgments

GETTING THIS BOOK INTO the hands of parents was a dream of mine long before I started writing it. For her role in making the dream come true I must first thank Betsy Lancefield Lane, former acquisitions editor for Contemporary Books, who saw the value of my message and took my proposal to the editorial board. Thank you, Betsy, for sharing my vision and for helping to launch this project.

When Betsy took a new job, the editorial reins for *Your Active Child* fell to Michele Pezzuti, who embraced the project with enthusiasm. Michele, thank you so much for allaying my concerns and answering all my questions. You're a delight to work with! Thanks, too, to Ellen Vinz for her careful and thoughtful editing.

I offer my sincerest gratitude to those friends and colleagues who so willingly gave their valuable time to review chapters and impart their expertise. They include Karen Baas, Charlene Burgeson of the Centers for Disease Control, Rhonda Clements, Marjorie Corso, Marinel Hartogensis, Bob Hautala, Rebecca Lamphere, Bill Yongue, and Judy Young of the National Association for Sport and Physical Education.

Huge hugs to Carolyn Parrott, who can count proofreading among her many talents and who so generously volunteered to read my chapters. I appreciate the gift of your time—not to mention all your invaluable suggestions! Thanks, too, to Peg Boyles, who recommended *Writing on Both Sides of the Brain* just as I was about to lose my mind (thanks, also, to the book's author, Henriette Anne Klauser), and to Chris Kenneally of the Copyright Clearance Center for his advice on promotion.

As always, my love and thanks go to friends Sheila Chapman and Patti Page, who, among other things, had to listen to me talk about this book week after week after week. To my husband, Richard Gardzina, who not only read but liked every chapter, I offer, as always, my heart.

Introduction

WE LIVE IN AN AGE of dichotomies. On the one hand we're bombarded with news reports of the ever-increasing obesity rates of children; on the other we see physical education programs disappearing from schools. We read and hear stories about children who simply don't go out to play anymore, and yet recess as part of the school day is going the way of the dinosaurs. We have children spending as much time watching television over the course of the year as they do in school and other children devoting eleven hours a week to participation in a single sport.

The last of these can be referred to as the "couch potato/superkid" dichotomy. Some children are participating in far too little physical activity; others are participating in too much. While parents may have heard that too little physical activity can be trouble, they may not at first see a problem with too much. But stories of early burnout abound. And whether we're talking about children who lose their early natural love of movement due to lack of physical activity or due to inappropriate kinds or amounts of physical activity, the end result is often the same: adolescence and adulthood *without* physical activity—and all the potential health problems associated with that.

In Chapter 1, "The Bad News About Couch Potatoes," I outline some of these health hazards. They include obesity (with its corresponding dangers of high blood pressure, stroke, and diabetes), cardiovascular disease, and cancer. In fact, a 1993 study showed that only tobacco causes more deaths per year than the nearly three hundred thousand deaths brought on by inactivity and poor nutrition.

I admit it: the intent of Chapter 1 is not only to inform you but also to scare you—to get you to think about the choices you and your child make relative to how he spends his free time. Does he spend it in front of the television set? Would he rather play computer games than backyard games? Will he become a statistic—one of the many children showing heart disease risk factors at an unnaturally early age?

With Chapter 2, "The Bad News About Superkids," I also hope both to scare and to inform. I want you to understand the dangers inherent in letting your child fall into today's "superkid" trap. Although the superkid syndrome in general causes children much harm (and we'll review why), the focus in this chapter is on expecting too much too soon in the area of sports.

I realize my stance on organized sports may prove to be unpopular with a number of parents. After all, the trend these days is to get children enrolled on a team practically from the time they're able to take their first steps without falling down.

Please know I have nothing against sports in general. I spend Sunday afternoons during football season jumping up and down and cheering like the most enthusiastic of sports fans. But the emphasis on sports and competition in our society has gotten out of hand and has no place in the lives of children under eight—the children who are the focus of this book.

Also, I've been a children's movement specialist for twenty-three years, and I've witnessed what they can and cannot do—what they are and are not capable of—physically, socially, emotionally, and cognitively. It is my position that children under the age of eight are not yet ready to play organized, competitive games. And I agree wholeheartedly with Shane Murphy, author of *The Cheers and the Tears,* when he writes, "As a vehicle for sponsoring mass participation in physical activity, youth sports programs are a huge failure."

If we really want our children to be physically fit and develop their motor skills so they have the ability, the confidence, and the desire to participate in lifelong physical activity, sticking them in right field or the backfield or on a soccer field as young children simply isn't the answer.

What is? Physical activity that's appropriate to a child's age and stage of development.

In Chapter 3 I give you the good news: all the ways in which developmentally appropriate physical activity can benefit your child. And it's not just in physical ways, although there's plenty of that. No, movement and active play have much to offer children in the social/emotional domain, contributing to, among other things, confidence, self-concept, and the ability to interact with others. And, believe it or not, movement and play are absolutely essential to your child's cognitive development. We'll explore some of the latest brain research demonstrating the links between moving and learning. Why do you need to know this stuff? So you can make well-informed choices for your child. So you can ensure a future that's as healthy—in every aspect of life—as possible.

When is the time for you to start thinking about such things? Well, why not at the same time you begin looking ahead to other important facets of your child's life, like her first doctor's appointments and her first words? Why shouldn't physical activity receive the same consideration as the food she eats, when both are components of health and fitness? Why shouldn't the education of her body (her motor development) be given the same priority as the education of her mind (cognitive development)?

With that in mind, I've opened Part II with a chapter on movement in infancy. While "earlier is better" may be a myth in a number of areas (flash cards and infant software come to mind), it is key to promoting physical health, proper motor development, and a lifelong love of physical activity.

This is not to say I'm advocating a "superbaby" approach. Rather, as you'll see in Chapter 4, I want you to understand the importance of movement beginning in infancy, because too many of today's babies are spending more time in playpens, high chairs, and car seats than in physically exploring their world. I want you to know the consequences of this trend. But I also want to warn you of the dangers of baby bouncers and walkers, which seem like such a good idea from a physical standpoint, and of the falsehoods involved in giving babies a "head start" by enrolling them in infant swim and exercise programs.

In Chapters 5 and 6 we look at what you can do—sensibly—to help promote your child's motor development and fitness, respectively. Motor skills may develop naturally in most children, but as you'll learn in Chapter 5, maturing chronologically doesn't ensure that an individual's motor skills will also reach maturation. On the contrary, instruction and practice are needed if a child's performance level and movement "vocabulary" are to increase. And early childhood—the span from birth to eight according to the National Association for the Education of Young Children—is the best time for such practice and instruction to occur. It's also during these years that habits are formed and attitudes shaped. That's why it's the best time to introduce your child to developmentally appropriate fitness.

With Chapters 7 and 8 I address two topics that are the subjects of much heated debate in today's society: physical education and recess. Anyone who's ever hidden in the background during "gym" class wonders why children should be subjected to the physical and emotional pain it can inflict. And with everything children need to learn in school, why should they be spending valuable time in either physical education *or* recess? There are more good reasons than I could tell you, but I've detailed as many as I possibly can in these two chapters.

Finally, while each of the first five chapters in Part II ends with suggestions for what you, as a concerned parent, can do, the last chapter is pretty much devoted to what you can do. The title of Chapter 9, "Preparing Your Child for a Lifetime of Physical Activity," pretty much says it all.

I know parents only want the best for their children. Unfortunately, many parents honestly believe that early sports participation *is* the best—or they remain unaware of the very real dangers of inactivity. Perhaps they're not even aware of just how inactive their children are. Most of us ran and climbed and biked as children. We didn't have to worry about getting enough exercise; just being a kid was enough! So we assume it's the same for our children. But it isn't. Things have changed and, unfortunately, not for the better. That's why I was determined to write *Your Active Child*.

For too long in our society, the functions of the mind have been considered superior to the functions of the body. I want to help change that attitude. I want you to put this book down with a new appreciation for the importance of developmentally appropriate movement in *every* aspect of a growing child's life. I want you to understand there is no dichotomy between mind and body; the functions of one contribute to the functions of the other. In fact, when you finish reading this book, you'll understand that movement and active play contribute not only to your child's physical development but also to her or his social/emotional and cognitive development—to what early childhood professionals describe as development of the whole child.

Part I

WHAT YOU NEED TO KNOW

I

The Bad News
About Couch Potatoes

"What a disgrace it is for man to grow old without ever seeing the beauty and strength of which his body is capable."

—SOCRATES

IT SEEMS YOU CAN'T open the newspaper these days without reading about the abysmal state of children's fitness. A sampling of recent headlines pretty much tells the story:

- "Heart Disease Begins in Childhood"
- "As Children's TV Time Rises, So Do Obesity Rates"
- "Growing Up . . . and Out: American Kids Heavier Than Ever"
- "Kids Urged to Turn Off TV & Go Play: Couch-Potato Lifestyle Blamed for Obesity Epidemic"
- "Obese Children Bound for Lifelong Health Problems, Experts Warn"

What's going on here? How can obesity be such a problem in childhood? After all, most of us probably remember knowing only one or two "fat kids" the whole time we were young. Now they're talking about a childhood obesity *epidemic*? And *heart disease*? Surely that must be a mistake. Although nowadays we do sometimes hear about people in their thirties and forties

3

having heart attacks (as opposed to the "good old days" when only people in their sixties and older suffered such fates), it seems absolutely preposterous that we should now be worrying about the hearts of children!

Unfortunately, it's all too true. And that's not even the whole story. As you'll learn in this chapter, there is much cause for concern about the health of today's children, about their future, and about the future of children to follow. In fact it may already be too late to prevent the occurrence of health risk factors in some of today's adolescents. However, if we smarten up now, it won't be too late for today's infants and young kids or for future generations.

But, you may be thinking, *my child isn't obese or overweight. It's a shame that other children are, but it's really not my problem.*

You would think not. But here are the facts: the estimated annual cost of obesity in the United States is about $100 billion—$127 million of which is related to obesity in children aged six to seventeen. This impacts health care and insurance costs for all of us. And even children who aren't obese or overweight can be unfit—and therefore at risk—if they're leading sedentary lifestyles.

But, you maintain, *young children are anything but sedentary. They're always moving!*

Well, they may be the most active segment of our population, but let's look at that a bit more closely. According to the surgeon general and the Centers for Disease Control and Prevention, 60 percent of adults don't take part in enough physical activity to benefit their health, and almost 30 percent get no physical activity at all. In other words we're a population of couch potatoes; so it really isn't saying much when we contend our children are our most active segment. And always moving? Not anymore. Would you be surprised to learn that the only activity children do more than watch TV is sleep? Read on for more startling information.

Why Just Being a Kid Is No Longer Enough

It's certainly understandable if you're having trouble wrapping your mind around this news. After all, with everything we have to worry about for our children, their getting enough exercise shouldn't even be on the list. Don't children, just by virtue of being children, move enough? Really, it may seem that way. But that could be because, with everything we have to get done these days, it feels as if the children are always underfoot—or on our nerves—keeping us from getting through the to-do list. After all, we have full-time jobs, homes to clean, laundry to do, groceries to buy, spouses requiring our attention, kids to shuttle hither and yon. And through it all we are forever admonishing the youngest of our children to sit still, stop their squirming, and not run. Certainly, it feels as if they're moving too much! But fidgeting, squirming, and the occasional burst of speed down a supermarket aisle can't even be considered minimal.

Of course, another explanation for this misconception about children being constantly on the move is that, given our own childhoods, we may simply equate being young with being perpetually in motion. If so, we might just be imagining our children are active enough. (One study showed that parents consistently rated their children as more active than teachers did even though there was no evidence the children's activity levels were actually higher at home.) So, if your initial response to the concept of sedentary children was "That's not possible. When I was a kid . . . ," maybe you need to consider the issue a bit further.

It's true that, once upon a time, children ran and skipped, climbed trees, jumped rope, played hopscotch, and rode their bicycles for blocks. Most likely you remember some of that yourself. Before you were old enough for school, it seems you were never indoors. You and the neighborhood children ran screaming through each other's yards and even down the middle of the streets. You raced each other to the slide and the swings, chased butterflies, and got filthy rolling around on the ground.

Then, once you were in school all day, the instant the bell sounded, you ran all the way home, shed your good clothes, and were out the door again. You played touch football, hide-and-seek, and tag. And you stayed outside until forced to come in. It's no wonder no one ever worried about your getting enough exercise!

But does all that activity bring to mind what your own children are doing? Probably not. Today's children are often in child care from the time they're infants. At the very least they start "school" at age three or four. Their days are organized for them practically from dawn to dusk. And they don't walk—let alone run—to and from school. Either they take buses or their parents drive them. (Parents drive kids *everywhere* these days.) Once home, even preschool and kindergarten children are expected to do homework now; so if it's not already dark by the time they get home, they have to use up what daylight is left getting their schoolwork done. (We got to enjoy childhood when we were children, and we turned out all right. Why is it we're so convinced our children will fail unless they start "rehearsing" for adulthood before they even know how to dress themselves?) Naturally, school-age children have even more homework—once they've fulfilled their many after-school obligations, like sports teams, dance class, gymnastics, and karate. (More about all that in the next chapter.) And even if they're not involved in all that stuff, there are plenty of other factors keeping them—and their younger counterparts—from just plain moving these days.

During the school day, for example, where once there were two or three recess periods providing opportunities to expend energy, children nowadays have maybe fifteen minutes of free time or none at all—because recess supposedly doesn't offer children as much as those other three Rs. (See Chapter 8 for more on this topic.) And physical education? That's being cut due to budget constraints and a nationwide fixation on "academic accountability" that's trickling down even to the preschool level. (Chapter 7 offers arguments as to why children need physical education in both early childhood settings and elementary schools.)

And, of course, movement in the classroom is generally forbidden (children who have a tendency to move in classrooms are all too often labeled hyperactive and prescribed Ritalin). As mentioned, even in preschool programs, which once offered young children a chance to learn through play, early childhood professionals are being caught between what they know about how young children learn and pressure from parents to concentrate on "preparing children for first-grade academics."

In one study researchers observed a classroom of preschool children (normally the most active of kids) for a period of six hours, during which the mean activity scores ranged from 1.96 to 2.42 and no sustained periods of Level 3 activity could be found. Even during a thirty-minute session of free play, the most active children didn't attain a mean rating of 3. The punch line is that Level 3 was equal to a moderate level of activity, like a slow walk! With the exception of moving from one activity to another, the most movement observed during this six-hour period was the wiggling of children in their chairs.

Once the regular school day ends, even those children not signed up for extracurricular activities—or without a lot of homework—don't have the opportunity to play like we did. Some are enrolled in after-school programs so they don't have to be home alone. Many of these programs, due to the large numbers of children involved, prefer to offer sedentary activities like arts and crafts, as opposed to body-moving ones. Those children who do go home *are* often home alone and have been instructed to remain indoors. Since children forced to stay inside are unlikely to do a lot of heart-pumping activity, or even to put on a CD and dance, the only after-school movement likely is that from the couch to the refrigerator and back again.

Then, of course, there's the space factor. Should they somehow have the time and the opportunity, most children don't have the wide-open fields, the empty lots, and the traffic-free streets we played in as kids. And even if there are playgrounds nearby, according to the National Program for Playground Safety, public playgrounds are often not what they ought to be in terms of design, maintenance, and supervision. All of this means that should the children venture outdoors, there's no room to roam. Nor do their parents want them to! Fears of abduction and dangers too frightening to imagine have parents keeping a tight rein on their young children these days. David Elkind, author of *The Hurried Child*, contends that today's children are no more at risk than their predecessors but that "thanks to television, we learn about every violent or obscene crime against children in alarming and graphic detail." Still, parents wonder, if there's even a remote possibility, why risk it?

Finally, there's the matter of competition for the child's attention. As you're probably aware, unlike when we were growing up, it's pretty fierce these days.

What Just Being a Kid Means Today

The short answer is: electronics. Handheld electronic games. Computers and computer games. Videos and video games. And, of course, television. That's what today's childhood entails.

Sure, we had television when we were kids. But there weren't as many channels to choose from. The reception might've been lousy. Our parents allowed us to view only one or two select programs. And, besides, we wanted to go out and play!

Today children spend the better part of their waking lives watching television. In fact, it's been estimated that between the ages of two and seventeen American children spend an average of *three years* of their waking lives watching TV (this doesn't even include time spent watching videos, playing video games, or using the computer). That's the equivalent of more than fifteen thousand hours in front of the set (about a thousand hours a year)—as compared with twelve thousand hours spent in a classroom. The end result? A total of twenty-seven thousand hours—more than six years of their young lives—without a whole heck of a lot of movement.

Perhaps most disturbing is how early it all starts—how entrenched in the habit children become before they're even preschoolers. Take a moment to absorb these facts gathered by pediatricians and other researchers from a study of 2,858 children who were part of the National Longitudinal Survey of Youth.

- Seventeen percent of infants under age one and almost half of the toddlers under two watch at least one hour of TV a day.
- One in four children under the age of three—and 41 percent of two-year-olds—are in front of the TV at least three hours each weekday.
- Ten percent of one-year-olds and 16 percent of two-year-olds are watching television for five or more hours a day.

According to the American Academy of Pediatrics (AAP), when television viewing becomes habitual for children ages birth to three, it's a practice that tends to last. In fact, two-year-olds who watch too much TV are two and a half times more likely to watch an excessive amount by the time they're six.

As appalling as these statistics are, they're unfortunately not all that surprising. Many child-care settings have TVs available. Children home alone after school often opt for the company of the box—and there's no one to tell them they can't. Also, as mentioned, parents are busy these days. The television keeps children "busy, happy, and good"—in other words, out of adults' hair. And watching television is a national pastime, with Americans in general spending 40 percent of their leisure time in front of the tube. By the time the average person hits age seventy, he or she will have spent about seven to ten years watching TV. Children do follow the lead of the role models in their lives.

In 1999 the AAP issued a policy statement suggesting that children under age two not be allowed to watch TV because "babies and toddlers have a critical need for direct interactions with parents and other significant caregivers for healthy brain growth and the development of appropriate social, emotional, and cognitive skills." (See Chapter 4 for more on this topic.) While parents can certainly see the validity of this statement, many of them were nonetheless displeased with the guidelines. They wondered how they were supposed to make dinner if their infants and toddlers weren't allowed to watch TV. But as Dr. Michael Rich, a pediatrician at Children's Hospital in Boston, points out, parents still had to cook dinner fifty years ago, and they had no television to provide a distraction. He says: "It's so enmeshed in our society and our patterns that we don't have the imagination to know how else to do it."

On the other hand, Robert Sachs, president of National Cable Television, contends that denying children TV is no more likely to encourage them to enjoy other activities, like reading, than denying them ice cream would encourage them to like brussels sprouts. What Mr. Sachs fails to consider, however, is that if there were no television to fall back on, children would have to find something else to do. We did, didn't we?

Sadly, these days that "something else" could well involve something else electronic. One study reported that children spend approximately thirty-three hours a week being electronically entertained (including but not exclusive to television)—an average of nearly five hours a day. Another, in 1999, found that children spend an average of six hours and thirty-two minutes a day with various media combined! It's unlikely the situation has improved since then.

Video games, once almost exclusively the entertainment of adolescents, have become popular fare for preschoolers as well. And the trend is growing. It seems everyone from "Sesame Street" (Elmo alone had at least four at last count) to the "Teletubbies" to "Blue's Clues" is marketing video games for preschoolers. And just try to lure the little ones away from them once they've gotten hooked!

Then, of course, there are the computers. Without a doubt, computers are an invention most of us can no longer imagine living without. But there's a great deal of controversy regarding the age at which children really need to begin using them. Alison Armstrong and Charles Casement, authors of *The Child and the Machine: How Computers Put Our Children's Education at Risk*, tell us computers and television have more in common than is generally acknowledged. Both, they say, involve individuals sitting motionless before a screen that feeds them "a rapid succession of images." They add: "Both computers and television present us with an artificial world that undermines our ability to experience the real one. We should bear this in mind when contemplating the possible effects of computer use on young children."

Naturally this isn't the place to delve into the ill effects of computer use on children under the age of eight. For the purposes of this chapter, *motionless* is the key word. Whether staring at a computer or a television screen, the children are sedentary. And they're not just plopped in front of computers at home either; more and more class time is being spent at computers, in lieu of learning that uses a variety of senses.

In 1929, writing in *The Aims of Education*, Alfred North Whitehead stated: "I lay it down as an educational axiom that in teaching you will come to grief as soon as you forget that your pupils have bodies." No one, it seems, took note. Seventy-five years later, were he writing in a publication for parents, he might well issue a similar warning for them and their offspring.

The High Cost of Being a Couch Potato

Remember lying on your back outdoors and finding creatures in the clouds? Remember making up scenes to act out, where maybe you were a pirate, a pilgrim, or a police officer? Did you daydream about your future and the possibility of becoming a veterinarian, a firefighter, or an astronaut?

Now imagine that, instead of doing all that imagining, you spent your time watching someone *else's* images—those of TV producers, software designers, and the creators of video games. They're vivid and compelling and amazing—and sometimes it's hard to believe they're not real. There's absolutely no need to create images in your own mind when you have so many incredible ones at the touch of a finger.

If you'd spent your childhood in this manner—without making use of that active imagination we take for granted in children—do you suppose you'd be able to get it to kick in on command when you needed it as an adult? That you'd easily be able to imagine the solution to a problem or challenge faced? That you could imagine what someone else's pain or joy felt like? That you could create an image of what you want in life? Why should the imagination not be subject to the notion of "use it or lose it"?

In Chapter 8 we'll look more closely at the importance of creativity and the imagination. But, for now, if you agree the loss of imagination could be a harsh price to pay for couch-potatoism—albeit an intangible one— you'll find the other costs (the more "concrete" ones) even harder to accept. Let's look first at the truth about television viewing, simply because it is the most sedentary activity in which children engage.

The truth is: too much television results in an unfit individual—adult or child. Kenneth Cooper, author of *Fit Kids!*, reports that in 1998 researchers at San Diego State University found that both parents' and children's performance levels on a simple test of aerobic fitness (one-mile walk/run) decreased as their TV viewing increased. Cooper says simply that children who watch several hours of television every day have lower fitness levels than those who watch fewer than two hours. Considering that in 1989 only 32 percent of children ages six to seventeen met the minimum standards for cardiovascular fitness, flexibility, and abdominal and upper-body strength— and sedentary behavior has only increased since then—this is definitely not good news.

Worse still, as the hours spent watching TV increase, so does the likelihood of obesity among children and adolescents. Researchers are discovering that the percentage of body fat increases along with the number of hours spent in front of the tube—and that obesity is lowest among children who watch television for one hour or less a day. In fact the risk increases almost 2 percent for each additional hour watched. With over 25 percent of children watching at least four hours a day, the potential for disaster is easy to recognize.

The formula is pretty straightforward: energy in/energy out. This is the term nutritionists use to describe the intended balance between calories consumed and calories burned. If the level of physical activity is not great enough to burn the amount of calories taken in, weight increases. If this imbalance continues, overweight and possibly obesity result.

Of course we're all aware that obese children suffer psychologically and socially. What you may not be aware of is that an individual's body image is pretty well established by the age of six. It may also come as a surprise that overweight children, like overweight adults, face discrimination—even among themselves. In one study, six-year-olds were shown silhouettes of different people and then asked to describe them. Regardless of their own body size, the children consistently conferred negative labels when presented with a silhouette of a heavy child, using such words as *stupid, slow, lazy,* and *dirty.*

Perhaps even more appalling, in yet another study teachers were found to equate beauty with brains. In this study different teachers were given the same student file consisting of much diverse information, including grades in the various content areas, attitudes and work habits, and a tally of absences. The only difference among the files distributed was the "student photo" attached to each. The teachers' analyses showed that they believed the attractive boys and girls were "more intelligent, more likely to get advanced degrees, able to get along better with other children, and to have parents more interested in their education." The "unattractive" children were consistently rated lower in these and other areas—even though all of the factual information was exactly the same.

It's no surprise, then, that the self-image and self-esteem of overweight children are generally quite poor. And this is only exacerbated by the teasing and ridicule of their peers—a situation that, in these post-Columbine days, can result in much more than hurt feelings. Even if children aren't tormented into taking their frustration out on others, they may well take it out on themselves. In 1994 an Associated Press article told the story of eleven-year-old Brian Head, an overweight child who shot and killed himself as a last resort against the ridicule of his classmates. Growing up can be difficult enough; growing up feeling isolated can be too much to handle.

Then, of course, there are the many physical consequences of obesity. In the United States, tobacco causes approximately four hundred thousand deaths a year. Diet and inactivity are to blame for three hundred thousand. According to the U.S. surgeon general in his 2001 Call to Action, death from obesity may now be as common as death from poverty, smoking, or problem drinking. He warns that a significant increase in the risk of disease can be attributed to even a modest weight gain. (For example, a gain of only eleven to eighteen pounds increases a person's chance of developing Type 2 diabetes to twice that of those who haven't gained weight.) In fact, people who are obese have a 50 to 100 percent increased risk of premature death from all causes compared to individuals who aren't obese.

The health risks of obesity are indeed numerous—with many risks coming as a surprise to most people. We realize, of course, that heart disease can be caused by high blood pressure and/or high cholesterol, both of which can result from poor diet and lack of physical activity. Stroke is also commonly understood to be a possible result of obesity.

But did you know that many cancers (colorectal, prostate, breast, endometrial, cervical, ovarian, gallbladder) are also on the list of health risks for the obese and overweight? Dileep G. Bal, president of the American Cancer Society, maintains that at least one-third of all cancers can be attributed to poor diet, physical inactivity, and overweight. This is higher than any cause other than tobacco.

Additionally, over the past twenty years, gallbladder disease in children has tripled and sleep apnea (resulting from extra folds of flesh in the throat obstructing airways) has increased fivefold. Both are obesity-related illnesses.

Here, in a nutshell, are some of the other health risks of overweight and obesity:

- Diabetes (insulin resistance, hyperinsulinemia)
- Respiratory disorders
- Decreased release of growth hormone
- Osteoarthritis
- Gout
- Musculoskeletal disorders
- Fatty deposits in the liver, leading to inflammation
- Early maturation
- Orthopedic problems

It's not a pretty list. But the scariest part may be that many of the unsafe behaviors (such as eating poorly and engaging in a sedentary lifestyle)—

and a number of the risk factors—begin in childhood. Type 2 diabetes was formerly known as *adult-onset* diabetes, as it was previously unheard of among the young. It is now seen in record numbers among the young (the incidence of Type 2 diabetes has almost doubled over the last twenty years). And early onset of diabetes will most likely mean its complications also begin earlier in life. When adults develop Type 2 diabetes, they suffer complications at about age fifty; children with Type 2 diabetes can expect to see complications at about age twenty. (We currently spend approximately $96 billion annually treating diabetes in the United States, mostly due to its complications.)

And heart disease? As mentioned at the beginning of the chapter, this is no longer a concern of senior citizens only. Nor should we wait until middle age to start thinking about it! Whereas in the past heart disease risk factors were rarely seen in anyone under the age of thirty, today it's becoming all too common to find them in children and adolescents—even those without a history of heart disease in their families. Studies have shown that 40 percent of children ages five to eight have at least one risk factor, including hypertension. (Should we be using the words *five-year-old* and *hypertension* in the same sentence?) The first signs of arteriosclerosis ("hardening of the arteries") are also now appearing at age five. According to the Centers for Disease Control and Prevention (CDC), the Bogalusa heart study, the longest and most detailed study of children in the world, found that 58 percent of overweight children had at least one additional risk factor for cardiovascular disease, and more than 20 percent had two or more risk factors.

In another study, Dr. E. Murat Tuzcu, director of the Intravascular Ultrasound Laboratory at the Cleveland Clinic Foundation, and colleagues looked at the arteries of 181 transplant recipients whose hearts were harvested from donors ages thirteen to fifty-five, all of whom had died not from disease but in car accidents or from gunshot wounds. These researchers discovered that one in six hearts from teenage donors had significant blockages (plaque) in at least one coronary artery delivering blood to the heart. Had they not died in accidents, following decades of plaque formation, these donors would have been likely candidates for heart attacks at fifty, forty, or even thirty.

The moral of the story is: most of the chronic and deadly diseases of adulthood don't just suddenly *appear*. They start early and develop quietly. When we finally learn about them, it's usually too late to do anything about them.

The CDC tells us that chronic diseases account for seven of every ten deaths in the United States and for more than 60 percent of our medical costs. Further, the lingering illness and disability common to many chronic diseases reduces the quality of life for millions of Americans. Today's most common chronic disease in the United States? It's obesity.

Not Our Problem?

Economist John Kenneth Galbraith has said that more people die in this country of too much food than of too little. It's an appalling notion—but an accurate one. As of 1999 more than 60 percent of American adults were overweight or obese—and obesity among children was increasing faster than among adults. In 2000, 22 percent of U.S. preschoolers were overweight and 10 percent clinically obese. Twenty-five percent of Canadian children are considered overweight. And a 2002 report in the *British Medical Journal* states that one in five nine-year-olds is overweight and one in ten is obese.

Nevertheless, there are many who consider obesity an individual responsibility. Writing in the *Los Angeles Times* in December 2001, Brian Doherty ridiculed former surgeon general David Satcher's "fat war." He called on taxpayer-funded agencies to think twice about spending Americans' money to lecture us on what he considers a matter of private health. He believes obesity is a condition "caused by freely chosen behavior" and maintains people can simply cure themselves of obesity by eating less and exercising more.

Fair enough. Everyone's entitled to an opinion. But you have to wonder if Mr. Doherty has done any research on the issue—or if he's simply speaking as someone who personally has a handle on his own "love handles." If it's the latter, he's to be congratulated for his self-discipline—but rebuked for not digging a little deeper as a journalist (and/or for his lack of empathy). After all, if the majority of people in this country have a weight problem, we need to look into the reasons why. If there are now nearly twice as many overweight children and almost three times as many overweight adolescents as there were in 1980—and it previously took thirty years for the number of overweight American children to double—we have to admit that something, somewhere, is very wrong.

Certainly we all wish the problem would just disappear—that it wouldn't be our problem at all. Who at one time or another hasn't wished for a simple solution to the predicaments that plague us? In this case, if everyone just took personal responsibility for her or his own weight gain, we wouldn't have to spend $100 billion dealing with obesity. And there's no doubt that personal responsibility is a *good* thing. But David Satcher tells us this is "the most overweight, obese generation of children in our history." Exactly whose responsibility is that? Let's think about it.

Without even taking into consideration the $100,000 paid to schools by soft drink companies to fill our children's bodies with empty calories, there's still the issue of recess and physical education disappearing from the schools. Who's making the decisions to eliminate all physical activity from the school day (where children spend most of their waking hours) despite mounting evidence that children need to move—for the health of both their bodies and their minds? (More on this later in the book.) Not the children. Given a choice, they'd happily choose to mix some movement into the day.

There's also the matter of loading children's days with activities that *preclude* "exercising more." Given a choice—and the opportunity—children might well opt to spend more of their time running, jumping, and breathing hard. But they're not being allowed to "choose freely." Rather, adults are choosing for them—the very adults who are supposed to know what's best for them and who have been entrusted with their care and protection.

Are the children responsible for the fact that 32 percent of two- to seven-year-olds—and 65 percent of eight- to eighteen-year-olds—have TVs in their bedrooms? Is it their fault they're not born with self-limiting mechanisms—and that too often parents have forgotten how to say no? If young children were able to set their own limits with regard to television viewing and computer and video use, they'd need parents only to provide food, clothing, and shelter.

The problem is, once a child is obese because of all of these adult-made decisions, the odds are pretty much stacked against him. Not only are behavior patterns, like eating and physical activity habits, established in childhood (educational psychologist Benjamin Bloom contended that 90 percent of an individual's habits and traits are set by age twelve), but long-term studies have also shown that excess body fat tends to persist throughout childhood and into adulthood.

And it's no wonder. Not only will "supersized" servings confront her at every turn, but also physical activity will become an even smaller part of the overweight child's life as she gets older. This is true of children in general (Kenneth Cooper reports that by age thirteen most boys and an even greater majority of girls take part in no regular physical activity at all) but is even more probable for the overweight child.

Many of us have nightmarish recollections of trying to climb the rope, or being forced to run laps until overcome with nausea, during "gym class." Surely any kind of physical activity would feel equally nightmarish to an overweight child. Even if they're inclined to move, overweight children are often physically incompetent. According to an article at the website of the International Play Equipment Manufacturers Association (IPEMA), during one study approximately 120 children ages three to ten were observed traversing an overhead ladder. The only children unable to cross the ladder successfully were obese. In another study it was determined that even children's walking patterns were affected by overweight, with obese children walking slower, asymmetrically, flat-footed, and with toes turned out. Over time these poor walking habits can result in structural deformities and damage to body tissue. And, of course, if even walking is a challenge, anything beyond that could be perceived as overwhelming.

Is it any surprise, then, that 40 percent of obese children and 70 percent of obese adolescents become obese adults? Indeed, by the time obese children are six years old, their chances of becoming obese adults are over *50 percent*. It's a vicious-circle kind of problem. Lack of physical activity is a primary cause of excessive fat accumulation in children. Then, once overweight, children have a tendency to become even less physically active—a tendency that only increases in adolescence.

Sure, Richard Simmons started out as a "fat kid" and managed to overcome the odds, but he's devoted his entire life to it! Not many individuals are likely to hand over the better part of their lives to rid themselves of excessive fat accumulation acquired before they were even old enough to understand the problem.

A Different Kind of Energy Crisis

Given our fondness for fast food (an ever-growing fondness, due to ever-busier lives) and our tendency to "supersize," it's easy to imagine that caloric *intake* is the crux of the obesity problem. And certainly it is part of the problem. (The biggest difficulty with that half of the energy in/energy out equation appears to be not with the number of calories consumed but with the *quality* of calories consumed. Recent evidence indicates that children get a full quarter of their vegetable servings in the form of potato chips and French fries!) But the greater problem lies with the second half of the equation: energy out.

Studies both here and abroad have indicated this is true. The Framingham Children's Study, for example, found that preschool children with low levels of physical activity gained significantly more subcutaneous (beneath the skin) fat than did more active children. In another it was determined that inactive preschoolers were 3.8 times more likely than active preschoolers to have increased triceps skinfold thickness (the best measure of obesity in children) in follow-up assessments. It's also been found that children who watch more than five hours of television a day are almost five times more likely to be overweight than children who watch two hours or less—with excessive TV viewing considered to contribute to 60 percent of the risk of obesity in children.

More specifically, in the United Kingdom, while the proportion of overweight or obese children remained the same between 1974 and 1984, there was a marked increase in the following decade. The research, reported in the *British Medical Journal*, determined the change was due not to increased energy (caloric) intake but rather to a decrease in energy *output*.

Studies in the United States have made the same determination. An increase in childhood obesity of 20 percent over the last decade (at least one in five American children is currently overweight) has occurred *despite* a decrease in overall fat consumption and little change in caloric intake.

Emphasizing Energy Out

In 2000, the *International Journal of Eating Disorders* reported the results of a study conducted at Stanford University School of Medicine in Palo Alto, California. The most disturbing findings of this study were that children as young as eight years old conveyed dissatisfaction with their body weight—and 16 percent of the eight- to eleven-year-olds surveyed had actually tried to shed pounds. Among their reasons for wanting to lose weight were wanting to look or feel better, being uncomfortable or embarrassed, receiving pressure from family members, and being teased by peers. Others have reported that by the fourth grade a full 80 percent of American girls have tried or are dieting.

Despite the escalating obesity problem, dieting is not an acceptable means of controlling weight in children. Although parents certainly want to ensure their children aren't subsisting on a regime of empty calories, reducing the fat content of children's food is neither necessary nor wise. Essential fatty acids have been thus named because they are indeed essential. When children are put on low-fat diets, they don't get the fats they need to grow properly. In fact, children need approximately twice as much fat as do adults.

Furthermore, studies show that dieting is often a prelude to eating disorders. An article on the WebMD site ("When Babies Watch What They Eat: Excessive Dieting Begins Over Baby Fat Fears") tells the story of Mindi Rold, whose battle with anorexia nervosa began at about age six, when she recalls being worried about having too much baby fat. By age nine Mindi was in a mental hospital. As a teenager she weighed sixty pounds.

Energy *out* is the key to maintaining an appropriate weight during childhood. As such, "exercise" should be a natural part of the child's daily life—a habit as common as brushing teeth. But it should always be about health—never about looks.

According to the authors of a research article appearing in the journal of the American College of Sports Medicine, there is one consistent observation that stands out among the studies of energy expenditure in young children. That unfortunate observation is that children under the age of seven seem to expend about 20 to 30 percent less energy in physical activity than the level recommended by the World Health Organization.

Sedentary children? Obese children? Unfit children? They're all a fact of life in today's society. The sad irony is that in today's society we're more "active" than ever—in terms of "busyness," that is. Perhaps we should get busy becoming more active in the physical sense.

Said Dr. Samuel Abbate, at a childhood obesity conference sponsored by the North Dakota Department of Health: "The consequences of denying the body exercise are just as severe as depriving it of food, water, or oxygen; it just takes longer to see the consequences."

In the second part of this book we'll look at the strategies you can employ to ensure that developmentally appropriate physical activity becomes a regular part of your child's life. Remember: the bad news is that there are three hundred thousand deaths a year in the United States alone due to low levels of activity and fitness. The good news is that they're due to *low levels of activity and fitness*—something that's extremely fixable.

2

The Bad News About Superkids

"Wrong ideas have a nasty habit of catching on, and clinging on, more easily than correct ideas. The belief that earlier is better in relation to early childhood is one such wrong idea."

—David Elkind

Like the childhood obesity problem, the subject of "superkids" gets plenty of press these days. *Time* devoted the better part of an issue to it. *Newsweek* featured an article entitled "Busy Around the Clock." Articles with titles like "Whatever Happened to Play?" "Pushing Children Too Hard," and "Are You Over-Scheduling Your Kids?" show up in print media and on the Internet. Books with titles like *Hyper-Parenting: Are You Hurting Your Child by Trying Too Hard?* are appearing on bookshelves.

What are superkids? Some call them *overscheduled*; others refer to them as *pushed* or *hurried*. Some speak of the practice of creating superkids as *scheduled hyperactivity*. Child development specialist David Elkind writes: "Parents are under more pressure than ever to overschedule their children and have them engage in organized sports and other activities that may be age-inappropriate." Most agree the practice is today's status symbol among families. In short, a superkid is a child pressured by parents and by society in general to do too much too soon.

Elkind's bestselling book, *The Hurried Child*, is subtitled *Growing Up Too Fast Too Soon*. Now in its third edition, the book has been bought by more than three hundred thousand people. One would therefore assume it's prompted considerable change over the twenty years since it was first published. Yet, in his latest preface, Elkind admits many of the problems he described in previous editions have only gotten worse.

All of this begs the question: if people are reading this stuff, why aren't they doing something in response to it? It seems, instead, they're simply ignoring all the warnings. As a result the phenomenon of superkids in our society is an escalating trend—with no end in sight. It's a frightening thought.

Writing in the magazine *Child Care Information Exchange*, Johann Christoph Arnold says: "The pressure to excel is undermining childhood as never before." He also asks: "Why are we so keen to mold [children] into successful adults, instead of treasuring their genuineness and carefree innocence?"

Ian Tofler and Theresa Foy DiGeronimo, authors of *Keeping Your Kids Out Front Without Kicking Them from Behind*, are even more plainspoken in their description of what's become of childhood. They write:

> In the process of trying to prepare our children for a rapidly evolving and fiercely competitive world, we too often professionalize and adultify our children by taking the fun out of childhood. We have turned summer camps into training camps where kids work hard to learn and improve useful skills. We have stolen lazy Saturday afternoons spent daydreaming under a tree and replaced them with adult-supervised, adult-organized activities and classes. We have taken our kids out of the neighborhood playgrounds and placed them in dance and music classes, in SAT preparation classes, and on organized athletic teams. There is no time that can be wasted on idle pastimes and on talent left unexplored or exploited.

We have the best intentions, of course. We want our children to be happy; we equate happiness with success. And we fervently believe that success won't come unless we give our children a head start—a jump on the competition as it were.

But at what cost will all of this "success" come? If children don't learn to play as *children*, they aren't likely to discover its value as adults. And, oh, what a dreary, deadening existence daily life will become. Think about the following questions, really pondering each for a moment:

- If children begin living like adults in childhood, what will there be left to look forward to?
- What's to ensure they won't be burned out from all the pushing and pressure before they've even reached puberty?
- If we've caused them to miss the magic of childhood, how will they ever find the magic necessary to cope with the trials and tribulations of adulthood?
- What will become of the childlike nature adults call on when they need reminding of the delight found in simple things—when they need to bring out the playfulness that makes life worth living?
- What joy will our children find as adults if striving to "succeed" becomes life's sole purpose?

Childhood is not a dress rehearsal for adulthood! It is a separate, unique, and very special phase of life. And we're essentially wiping it out of existence in an effort to be sure our children get ahead. But when did we decide that life was one long race? When, exactly, did life become a competition?

In this chapter we'll investigate the issue of superkids as it relates specifically to physical activity—as the opposite end of the spectrum from the couch potato problem. Yes, too little physical activity can have tragic results. But that doesn't mean the answer to the problem is too *much* physical activity! Although there may not be as many statistics to conclusively determine the negative effects of the superkid syndrome, pushing children to do too much too soon can be just as devastating as allowing them to do too little. We'll look at some of the consequences of involving children in competition and of allowing them to specialize in one sport before they're ready. And we'll explore the reasons that organized sports are not the means to either skill development or physical fitness. But first, let's look at some of the results, in general, of asking our kids to be superhuman.

Consequences of the Superkid Syndrome

For many adults getting through the day, day after day, can be like living in a pressure cooker. The demands on their time and energy are overwhelming, and it seems there's no time to breathe, let alone relax. Many of today's mothers, in particular, are feeling the strain of trying to be "Supermom"— trying to do and be it all: wife, mother, housekeeper, cook, chauffeur, and full-time career woman. Recent reports indicate that, while most women would not want to return to the days when choice wasn't an option for them, they're nonetheless unhappy with the way things stand. They're too tired to be happy. They've just plain had it.

So, doesn't it make you wonder? If adults are fried from the effects of living a too-full life, why would they want their children to be subjected to anything remotely like it? Having personally experienced the many nega-tive effects of trying to do too much in too little time—of living lives that are contrary to our nature—why are we not doing everything in our power to *protect* our children from a similar fate? Now more than ever, why aren't we doing all we can to ensure our children experience true childhood— while they have the chance?

David Elkind, in *The Hurried Child*, says that all children have "spe-cial needs," and ignoring them is no less unfair than failing to provide ramps for the disabled. We simply cannot ask our children to stop being children, any more than we can ask the blind to see.

Children are not small adults. They don't come equipped with the physical, social, emotional, and cognitive skills that adults possess. Yet more and more, parents are behaving as though they do. Still worse, they're ask-ing their children to handle lifestyles that even they, as adults, don't have the skills to handle. And, because children want so much to please their parents, they're complying. Because children want so much to please their parents, they very often participate in activities they don't like—or even that they hate. Because children want so much to please their parents, when their parents value accomplishment above all else—what the children are doing, rather than who they are—the pressure to accomplish is enormous.

Of course, there's nothing wrong with accomplishment per se. But is that really a word we want to be a dominant part of childhood? Isn't there plenty of time to focus on accomplishment in later years—say, when it has more meaning to the child herself? And what if the child isn't up to the task at hand—either because it's the wrong task or because she simply isn't devel-opmentally ready? The child fails. Research shows that, having failed once, a child is less likely to try a second time, even when it's possible the second attempt might well result in success.

Fred Engh, president of the National Alliance for Youth Sports and author of *Why Johnny Hates Sports*, has some strong words about adults imposing unrealistic expectations on children. He calls it emotional abuse, plain and simple, and says when it is "delivered during growth periods, the expectations and the standards may haunt the children for a lifetime. These are the ones who are going to be chronically unhappy with their lives, always unsatisfied and unfulfilled because they never did quite enough. Failure will dominate their existence and devastate their spirits."

Then there's the obligation factor. A great many children feel duty-bound to pay their parents back for any sacrifices in time and money they may have made on the children's behalf. But is *obligation* a feeling we want to be prevalent in our children's emotional lives?

Young children are not internally motivated to succeed; their only motivation comes from the value *you* place on success. And they don't want to let you down. As a result, stress is often a principal factor in the life of a superkid. Write Jim and Janet Sundberg, authors of *How to Win at Sports Parenting*:

> In striving for the success their parents demand, these individuals gradually accumulate the symptoms and signs of stress. In their twenties and thirties, for example, they develop chronic headaches or stomach problems—diarrhea, constipation, sour stomach. In their forties and fifties, they graduate to stomach ulcers, hypertension, panic attacks, and depression. No matter what they attain, they have learned, it will not be enough; they will have to strive for more.

Of course into every life a little stress must fall. But when it becomes more than a person is capable of handling, it becomes unhealthy. Studies have shown that the brains of stressed preschoolers now look remarkably like the brains of stressed adults, which have excessive levels of adrenaline and cortisol, the chemicals responsible for the body's fight-or-flight reaction. Young children, who don't have the vocabulary or understanding to express what they're feeling, will often act out as a way of coping. Sometimes the stress gets to be too much, and an eventual result is as drastic as teenage suicide.

But there's more than stress involved in pushing children onto the fast track to success before they even understand the concept. According to Elisabeth Guthrie and Kathy Matthews, authors of *The Trouble with Perfect*, when children aren't allowed to discover motivation on their own, they "never develop the imagination or the genuine internal sense of competence and motivation that they need to achieve real success as they grow older." And motivation, they say, is often more important to success than talent. We only have to recall some story heard—like the one about the too-small football player who made it big as a pro against all odds—to know this is true.

Moreover, these authors point to loss of connection with parents and an inability to discover oneself as further harm perpetrated on "pushed" children. One study involving children ages eleven to fourteen found that they longed for a greater sense of connection with their parents and more time to do things together. In another, 21 percent of the teenagers polled nationally said they were most concerned about the fact that they didn't have enough time with their parents. These were teenagers, mind you—individuals whom we normally think of as wanting to be as far away from their parents as possible! If they're feeling a lack, just imagine how younger children, who really need their parents' undivided attention but who can't yet articulate such thoughts, must be feeling. William J. Doherty, a professor of family social science at the University of Minnesota, maintains that if families don't make time for each other, the emotional connections will simply disappear.

And the inability to discover oneself? Guthrie and Matthews contend: "A pushed child has more difficulty finding who he is—what really interests him, what gives him pleasure—because he has been so undermined, consciously and unconsciously, by parents who have been working hard to produce the child they want or need rather than the child they have." The result, they state, is a partial identity formation that will cause real unhappiness as these individuals "struggle to become autonomous adults."

Another consequence for superkids is that they never learn to be at ease with themselves when alone, with time on their hands. Having experienced life "by the clock"—and almost constantly surrounded by others—these kids have never learned the joy of solitude, of having only oneself for company. Not only does this mean they're unable to practice self-reflection, but they're also unable to simply *be*. Without these abilities, an individual continues to feel constant pressure to produce, to do, to undertake! This is both exhausting and contrary to human nature. We are not Energizer bunnies; we were not meant to keep going and going and going. And we do need the wisdom and peace that comes from having an inner life.

Since the beginning of the last century, the rate of depression among individuals has grown with every decade. In 1999 an article in *Time* estimated that between five hundred thousand and one million prescriptions for antidepressants were being written annually for children and adolescents! Today it's estimated that 5 percent of adolescents, 2 percent of school-age children, and 1 percent of *preschoolers* suffer from clinical depression. Is it possible this is connected to our current expectations for kids?

Not long ago, in an attempt to help adults realize the folly of all work and no play, a saying began appearing on bumper stickers and in E-mails. It read: "No one ever said on his deathbed, 'I wish I'd spent more time at the office.'" Whether or not the saying had the desired effect remains to be seen, as adults appear as determined as ever to fill up their time with accomplishments. But someone had the right idea, and evidently quite a few people agreed with the sentiment. Isn't it now time to consider the same sentiment as it relates to children? Is there anyone who would say, at the conclusion of childhood, "I wish I'd had less time to play"? Who, after all, wants to look back on life and regret passing up that one and only opportunity to just be a kid?

Why Young Children Aren't Ready for Organized Sports

If there's one area where the practice of creating superkids is thriving, it's youth sports. Here children are encouraged (coerced?) to play adultlike games with adultlike rules (and, often, equipment), keeping adultlike, often grueling, practice and performance schedules. Here adults make nearly impossible demands on children—sometimes at the top of their lungs—and wonder, sometimes at the top of their lungs, why children don't meet

Organized Versus Pickup Games

Believe it or not, some of today's children have never played a good old-fashioned "pickup" game—a "sporting event" that happens spontaneously among children, with no adults in charge or in attendance. Following are some of the differences one can witness—or researchers have found—between the two. Which do you think is better for kids?

Organized Game	Pickup Game
• Intense competition—pressure to perform well—children anxious	• Children cooperating—no score kept—children relaxed
• Intense parents	• No parents (according to one study, preferable to children)
• Conflicts escalating out of control	• Conflicts resolved by children problem solving
• Mistakes made impact the game and the children's confidence	• Mistakes made result in "do-overs"
• Rules imposed without the children necessarily understanding them	• Rules invented—and reworked—as necessary
• Children sitting on the bench	• Everybody playing
• The sound of coaches and parents yelling	• The sound of children laughing

Have you ever heard the joyful sound of children's laughter during an organized game?

those demands to their satisfaction. Perhaps worst of all is the age at which all this craziness begins. Whereas organized competitive sports once truly were reserved for "youths," they are now the expected norm for children barely big enough to hold a bat.

But, you may think, *if lack of physical activity is bad and physical activity is good, it seems enrolling even very young children in organized sports is the answer parents are looking for.* But is it?

While more and more young children are taking part in sports such as soccer, hockey, and even jai alai, the goal isn't usually to give children an edge where physical fitness is concerned. Rather, parents sometimes believe that by placing their children in such programs, they're giving them a necessary *competitive* edge. And not just in sports but in life. After all, in our society, success in sports equates with success in life. Since parents feel a duty to prepare their children for the dog-eat-dog society they'll face as adults, even those who worry their children are too young for such activities are confronted with enormous pressure—from without and within—to enroll their little ones.

But what's the reality of the situation? Do organized sports promote motor development, thus giving young children an advantage over those who don't participate in them or who begin at an older age? And what *about* physical fitness? Won't playing T-ball or soccer or peewee football help ensure against all those frightening statistics cited in Chapter 1? We'll address these questions in the next section. But first, let's look at the young child's *readiness* for participation in organized sports, beginning with his cognitive development.

Between the ages of about two and seven years old, children are functioning at what noted child development expert Jean Piaget called the "preoperational stage of thinking." This means they're not yet able to think logically or abstractly and are able to handle only one aspect of a problem at a time.

In terms of sports, it means children aged two to seven are unable to decipher complicated coaching instructions, rules, or strategies. Additionally, during a game of soccer, for example, a preschooler will become so focused on dribbling that he'll be unable to even consider the possibility of passing the ball to a teammate. "One thought at a time" might well be the young child's credo, as is obvious to anyone who's ever witnessed what sports psychologist Shane Murphy calls "big clump soccer."

Added to this is what Kenneth Cooper, author of *Fit Kids!*, labels the "out-to-lunch syndrome" of the typical five-year-old, which causes her to be easily distracted and periodically lose interest in what's going on around her. Every parent who's ever attended a sporting event of a group of preschoolers has personally witnessed this syndrome, which Dr. Cooper assures parents is perfectly natural. He says that while a few children of this age may be reasonably focused and competitive, they are the exception rather than the rule.

Children under the age of eight also require time to think about the movements they want to make. That's because their decision-making abilities are noticeably slower than those of older children and adults. Thus they're not only performing movements more slowly than those who've had years of practice, but also they're taking more time to think about the movements!

Shane Murphy contends children simply aren't mentally equipped to handle sports strategies until the age of eleven or twelve and that too many adults make the mistake of expecting children to understand competitive sports from an adult's perspective. Kenneth Cooper asserts that children don't develop the concentration to focus on tactics until at least ten or eleven. And it's not until at least the age of nine that children are able to make a distinction between success/failure as the result of effort and success/failure as the result of ability. Before this, children are likely to believe their every failure is due to lack of ability—and that ability is something that can't be changed.

With regard to social/emotional development, according to Piaget, children aren't ready to cooperate or to take the perspective of another person until the age of seven or eight, when egocentrism (being centered on self) declines. In essence this means they're not able to understand the concepts involved in organized play and teamwork.

Steve Sanders, former editor of *Teaching Elementary Physical Education* and a professor with the Department of Health and Physical Education at Tennessee Technological University, relates the story of a soccer game for four- and five-year-olds that was as "developmentally appropriate as the league organizers could make it." Dr. Sanders reports that throughout the course of the game, there was much crying, especially when one child had the ball taken away by another. Although parents and coaches tried to explain this was part of the game, the children weren't developmentally ready to accept it.

Nor are young children emotionally ready to comprehend the investment in time and energy being asked of them. They don't "get" commitment; they just want to play! As Dr. Sanders says, placing preschool children in competitive sports situations is like placing a ten-year-old in a car and asking her to drive. She simply doesn't have the necessary skills.

And then there's the young child's physical development. We'll look again at the issue of children's developing bodies in the section on specialization in sports. But even if a child plays a variety of sports, the potential for injury should be a concern to every parent. After all, how much sense does it make to have adult games played by individuals with bodies that are anything but adult? By individuals whose muscles do not yet have their full volume or whose bones are not yet completely calcified?

The experts agree that it doesn't make much sense at all. The American Academy of Pediatrics has issued warnings on the subject. Dr. Kenneth Cooper cautions that contact sports such as football and hockey are too high-impact for the skeletal structure and organs of children aged eight and under. (Some collisions can cause irreparable damage.) He advises, additionally, that children of this age have inefficient mechanisms for ridding their bodies of heat, which makes such vigorous sports as soccer potentially dangerous.

Dr. Bob Rotella and Dr. Linda Bunker, authors of *Parenting Your Superstar*, warn that while a serious growth-plate injury to a fourteen-year-old can cause the loss of a quarter of an inch in height, the same injury to a seven-year-old can result in four or five inches of height lost! And Dr. David Elkind notes that children's bodies are configured differently from those of adults, pointing out that the head of a three- or four-year-old child is equivalent in size to a beach ball on an adult's body. This, along with other factors, means not only that a child will have greater difficulty performing adult sport skills but also that doing so may well place excessive stress on his body.

With regard to motor skills, by the time children are six years old they're generally able to run, jump, and bounce and catch a ball—all of which can be considered sport skills. Typically, however, preschool children haven't had the instruction, practice, and experience required to perform these skills at a *mature* level, which means they aren't likely to perform them well enough to be successful in sports. In fact, according to a study performed by the National Youth Sports Coaches Association, a full 49 percent of the eleven hundred five- to eight-year-olds surveyed were found to lack the ability to perform even the most fundamental skills required in their sports.

By the same token, eye-hand and eye-foot coordination usually aren't fully developed until the age of nine or ten. How, then, is a child of four or five to successfully connect bat to ball, stick to puck, or foot to moving soccer ball?

Seldom considered by those who put preschoolers into adultlike baseball or softball games is the matter of children's visual perception. Figure-ground perception—the ability to separate or distinguish an object from its surroundings—reaches maturity between the ages of eight and twelve. Depth perception—the ability to judge distance in relation to oneself—is generally not mature until age twelve. And visual-motor coordination—the ability to integrate the use of the eyes and hands in terms of object tracking—matures between ten and twelve. What this all boils down to is a heck of a difficult time catching a small white ball.

What About Sports' Alleged Advantages?

The prevailing belief, of course, is that sports participation will help improve physical skills—will help children acquire them more quickly. (Goodness knows, in today's society, we have to do everything more quickly!) But the facts don't support this belief. For one thing, some skills will simply not reach maturity until the child does. And, while placing children in situations allowing for instruction and practice of motor skills will indeed promote motor development, those situations aren't necessarily in the form of organized sports. On the contrary, several studies have demonstrated that competitive sports activities actually limit motor learning due to the scarce amount of genuine participation time involved.

Consider the following results of a variety of studies, reported by Steve Grineski in his book, *Cooperative Learning in Physical Education*:

- 75 percent of ball contacts were made by 40 percent of the players during a third-grade soccer game.
- 35 percent of players never caught the ball, while 52 percent of players never threw the ball during a fifth-grade kickball game.
- Three students never touched the ball or ran the length of the gym floor during a fifth-grade kickball game.

ITEM CHARGED

LIB#: *1000107225*
GRP: STUDENT

Due: 4/29/2009 08:00 PM

Title: Your active child : how to boost
physical, emotional, and cognitive
development through age-appropriate
activity / Rae Pica.
Auth: Pica, Rae, 1953-
Call #: 613.7042 PICA-R 2003
Enum
Chron
Copy:
Item *0039395T*

- Twenty third-grade children participating in a one-hour softball game had a total of thirty-nine throwing and catching opportunities. The average number of throwing and catching opportunities for each child for the one-hour game was 2.3.
- Children participating in an hour-long hockey game had possession of the puck less than two minutes each.

In other words, the children involved in these situations had very few opportunities to improve their throwing, catching, kicking, dribbling, or stick-handling skills. And these were elementary-school children! Younger children forced to play adult games without adult skills find they don't even know what they're expected to *do* when finally given an opportunity to perform.

But you don't need the results of studies to know this is true. If you've ever been to any organized contests involving young children, you've probably witnessed it yourself. There's the right fielder who grows so bored waiting for a ball to come her way that, by the time one finally does arrive, she's busy finding creatures in the clouds. Or the "wide receiver" who hasn't seen the football in so long he's forgotten what his job is and periodically just trots down the field and then back to the huddle. How, exactly, are these children supposed to be improving their skills?

In short, if traditional competitive sports programs don't provide children with the opportunities necessary to acquire, practice, and refine their motor skills, how likely is it that improved motor development will take place? And doesn't this also answer the question about improved physical fitness? If organized sports turn out to be nearly as sedentary as sitting on the couch, fitness certainly can't be the expected result!

But perhaps the more important questions are: If a child experiences more failure than success in organized sports, what happens to the love of movement she started life with? How likely is she to make physical activity an integral part of her later life?

The theory of flow, put forth by University of Chicago psychologist Mihaly Czikszentmihalyi, contends that people are happiest when the challenges they face are equal to the skills they possess. So what happens when the challenges presented to children are beyond their ability to succeed? Anxiety is one probable result. Another is the development of learned helplessness: the expectation, based on past experience, that one's every effort will lead to failure.

Motivation theorists have discovered that when failure is attributed to lack of ability and ability is considered beyond one's control, the cycle leads to embarrassment, withdrawal, and a decline in performance. And it makes perfect sense. What would your reaction have been if, as a child who hadn't yet "broken the code" of putting letters together to form words, someone insisted you read Shakespeare? What if, before you even knew how to add and subtract, your parents had urged you to try solving algebra problems? Chances are, you would have blamed yourself for your inabilities, concluded you would never master such tasks, and simply given up.

When we put children into situations for which they're not ready, we set them up for failure. And failure, of course, *feels* bad, which is the last thing we want for our kids. More significant, numerous studies have shown that negative early experiences with sports are a major factor in why kids quit participating in physical activity altogether. And then what happens to fitness? Hint: we end up breeding more couch potatoes.

Sure, there are exceptions to every rule. You may have an especially bright child who happens to grasp the complicated plays involved in his pee-wee football games. That doesn't necessarily mean he has the social skills required to cooperate with team members or to handle loss with dignity. Your daughter may be the epitome of grace and good sportsmanship on the playing field but be terrified at the sight of an oncoming ball due to undeveloped visual perception. In other words, it's highly unlikely that physical, social/emotional, and cognitive development will proceed at the same pace in a child.

And as to the question of early sports experience giving children a head start? You'll find more on this issue in Chapter 4. But, for now let's just say there's absolutely no evidence to show children who start early—before they're developmentally ready—have an advantage over those who begin when "all systems are go." Sure, children who begin earlier *may* learn certain skills earlier; but those children who begin when they're developmentally ready easily catch up and often even surpass those who started earlier. The American Academy of Pediatrics warns that "teaching or expecting these skills to develop before children are developmentally ready is more likely to cause frustration than long-term success in the sport."

There are two additional points to remember here. First, no one can *create* a superstar; either the giftedness and passion are there or they're not. And, second, if your child does happen to have been born with a special talent, there's no need to rush it; it won't have disappeared by the time he's eight!

The High Cost of Competition

Until now, we haven't even gotten into the issue of competition; and it is this issue, and the research behind it, that perhaps provides the strongest arguments against the young child's participation in organized sports. However, the subject of competition is one that provokes some pretty strong feelings in the United States. In fact, even hinting that competition might not be such a great thing can cause one to be labeled un-American.

Although we'll have to explore some generalities about competition, the intent here is not to determine whether competition is "good" or "bad." (Alfie Kohn has already done a quite thorough job of that in *No Contest*.) Rather, our purpose is to look at competition as it involves young children. Are they ready to understand and handle it? Does it contribute to their character? Will it help shape their future? Is it good *for them*?

The prevailing belief is that competition is good for everyone—that someone without a strong competitive nature is just a wimp. That someone who isn't fiercely competitive might just as well lie down and let the world walk all over him. That being competitive is human nature and to be non-competitive is to have been born without a necessary gene.

But is it human nature, or is it learned behavior? The research shows that, given a choice, most preschoolers prefer cooperative to competitive activities. This would seem to indicate that dog-eat-dog is not a natural inclination. And in a *New York Times* essay, Nicholas Kristof told a hilarious story about trying to teach the game of musical chairs to a group of five-year-old Japanese children, who kept politely stepping out of the way so others could sit in their chairs. This would certainly seem to indicate "dog-eat-dog" is *taught* in some societies—and not taught in others.

In our society the idea that competition is good, necessary, and inevitable "is drummed into us from nursery school to graduate school," says Alfie Kohn. These beliefs are promoted so regularly—in both subtle and not-so-subtle ways—that they're rarely questioned. Even if children were inclined to question a belief held so strongly by their parents and other role models, they don't possess the mental ability to do so until the damage is already done. No, children figure out early that their parents, teachers, and coaches want them to "eat or be eaten." Rewards—in the form of stars, good grades, trophies, applause, and lots of attention—are showered on winners. "Losers" get either no attention or the kind they don't want.

A 1999 European study found that when parents and coaches defined success as *winning*, as opposed to making an effort and showing progress in one's own performance, the athletes of these parents and coaches tended to feel the same way. This study points to the inevitability of children adopting the convictions of the role models in their lives, and it certainly seems to add credence to the theory that competition is learned.

Kohn tells us the research shows competition, among other things:

- Is not developmentally appropriate for young children and hurries them into adulthood
- Causes people to believe they're not responsible for what happens to them and contributes to the concept of learned helplessness
- Results in less spontaneity and creativity
- Significantly increases aggression
- Invites the use of cheating and other antisocial behaviors in order to win

Let's look at the last two points first. It's an almost unquestioned conviction in our society that sports—and, by extension, competition—build character. People can go on and on, expounding on the many values children supposedly learn by taking part in competitive sports. But the truth is, people have been parroting that sentiment for generations with very little research to support the theory. There is, however, evidence to the contrary.

Consider this: a 1995 poll of 198 Olympic or aspiring Olympic athletes, reported in *Sports Illustrated*, showed to what lengths individuals will go to win. Asked if they would take a banned, performance-enhancing substance that would both go undetected and enable them to win, 195 said they would; only three said no. And when asked if they would take such a substance if they would not get caught, they would win every competition entered for five years, and then die from the substance's side effects, more than half of the athletes said yes. Apparently, winning is more important than life itself.

But, you may be thinking, *those were athletes whose lives had revolved around winning for many years; they're probably an exception to the rule.*

Maybe, but the attitude had to begin sometime and grow from there, as this story indicates: a survey of 965 students at four middle schools in Massachusetts found that almost 3 percent of the children were using anabolic steroids to enhance their appearance and performance. From where do children as young as ten learn such skewed priorities?

Other research shows that long-term participation in sports results in the display of less sportsmanship and more aggressive behavior—and that even if athletes learn some prosocial behaviors on the field, they rarely transfer them to other areas of their lives. Studies have also demonstrated that competitive children are both less generous and less empathetic than others. Still, people continue to believe that sports participation builds character.

Is that the kind of "character" we want our children to grow up with? Do we really want them embracing the lesson of win-at-all-costs?

True character must be *taught*; it doesn't simply happen because we've enrolled our children in soccer or T-ball. And when other children are viewed as impediments to one's own success, prosocial behaviors are not the likely result.

Consider for a moment the traditional game of musical chairs, at which the Japanese children failed so miserably in Nicholas Kristof's story. In America we play this game in child-care centers, during play dates, and at almost every preschooler's birthday party. The rules say that a chair is removed with every round—and one more child gets to sit against the wall and watch everybody else continue to have fun. The game is over when there remains one winner—and lots of losers.

In case you don't recall from your own childhood (or maybe you were always the one winner among many losers), being eliminated feels lousy, as does feeling like a loser. And those other kids you're playing with? For the duration of the game they're not your friends; they're what's standing in your way. Children only have to play this game once to know that, if they're not going to be labeled losers, they have to do whatever it takes to win. And we've all seen what that means: punching, poking, kicking, scratching, screaming, and shoving—hardly the actions of someone with character. (See Chapter 3 for a description of cooperative musical chairs and its resulting, more character-driven, behaviors.)

When parents consistently place their children in situations where winning is the ultimate goal—where the winners are considered heroes and the losers "losers"—winning is what they come to value. They learn that only the end result counts, not the process involved in getting there. Further, when parents themselves fail to conduct themselves with character, their actions speak much louder than any words preached about good sportsmanship and the value of teamwork and cooperation.

In today's world *sideline rage* is a term familiar to us all. We've heard the stories demonstrating—and seen for ourselves—that when winning becomes what's most important, good sense and good behavior can get lost in the shuffle. And while all parents may not end up making the headlines (as did the "hockey dad" convicted of pummeling another father to death), any incidence of unacceptable behavior on the part of a parent can have a profound and lasting effect on a child. And it's not likely to be a good one. As the authors of *Hyper-Parenting*, Alvin Rosenfeld and Nicole Wise, point out, "It says a lot about our priorities that many parents today put more energy into teaching children how to serve a tennis ball than how to serve humanity."

Which brings us to an interesting point. While the goal of many parents is to give their children a running start on the development of sport skills (again, because success in sports certainly must equal success in life!), the research shows that competition is actually *detrimental* to skill development. One reason is fear of failure and its resulting stress, which isn't conducive to either learning or performance. Young children, in particular, are susceptible to this problem because pleasing their parents means so much to them. And when their parents focus on winning—either through action (screaming on the sidelines) or words (asking "Who won?" instead of "Did you have a good time?")—winning becomes the children's goal as well.

Of course, you may think the goal of winning would be enough to propel children into performing their best. But, remember, young children are not cognitively ready to make that connection. They attribute winning or losing to ability, not effort. Nor are they emotionally ready to handle the pressure of playing mistake-free games. And they're not physically ready to play without making mistakes! For them an emphasis on winning becomes fear of losing. And, as Christopher Andersonn, author of *Will You Still Love Me If I Don't Win?*, says, for young children, losing equates losing *love*—from parents, coaches, teammates, and sometimes the public in general.

But there are other reasons why competition hurts skill development. One is that, when winning is the goal, "less skilled" children are kept on the bench. We've already read the statistics about how few learning opportunities are available to the children who get to play. What happens to the skill development—and confidence—of the child who doesn't get to play or who is sent in for an inning as a gesture toward complying with the "everybody plays" rule?

And then there's the simple fact that concentrating on the execution of skills goes right out the window the moment competition is introduced. For example, video taken of kindergarten children asked to run the length of a gymnasium showed some children with quite a mature form: body straight and slightly leaning forward, arms moving in opposition to the legs, feet hitting the floor heel-ball-toe, eyes forward and focused. Then, with camera rolling, pairs of children were challenged to *race* one another across the length of the gym. The same children who'd demonstrated excellent form were now seen running flat-footed, with arms flailing and the upper torso leaning so far forward as to almost upset balance. Most significantly, instead of looking straight ahead, these children were now looking over their shoulders at their "opponents," which resulted in twisted hips and shoulders. As Alfie Kohn points out, "Trying to do well and trying to beat others are two different things."

Finally, when product (winning) is emphasized over process (making an effort), extrinsic reward is granted more validity than intrinsic reward. As a result, trophies and championships become the whole point of participation. And while this may not seem like such a bad thing in a goal-oriented society, we're back to the issue of the young child's stage of development. Children under the age of eight are motivated by pleasure. And, yes, winning feels good when everyone around you is making a big deal out of it. But does that feeling last?

And what about the children who aren't winning? As Jim and Janet Sundberg state, "If winning is the only way to succeed or to gain good things from sports, then half of all team members in any given season will be miserable failures."

As mentioned, children just want to play. In fact, one study asked children whether they'd prefer to sit on the bench for a winning team or play for a losing team. Seventy-eight percent chose the latter! Other studies have determined the number-one reason children want to play sports is to have fun—and that the number-one reason they quit is that it just isn't fun anymore. Indeed researchers have found that 73 percent of children who participate in organized sports quit by the age of thirteen due to negative experiences.

During a consultation for Children's Television Workshop (now Sesame Workshop), the former head writer of "Sesame Street" asked the question: "If children never lose, how will they learn to lose?" It's an interesting question—perhaps even one that's crossed your mind.

Yes, as children go through life, they will face situations when they lose—when they're less successful than someone else or less successful than they'd like to be. And, yes, they do need to know how to handle such situations. But is setting them up to lose, or fail, a *lot* the best way to teach them to cope? As mentioned, repeated failures lead to a sense of learned helplessness—the belief that one has absolutely no control over the happenings in one's life. Surely that's not a lesson we want our children to learn. Rather, if they have many more opportunities to experience success (not in terms of winning but in terms of enjoyable, positive experiences), what they will gain are poise and confidence. And aren't poise and confidence going to serve them better than learned helplessness when they're faced with a challenge, or with the reality of loss or failure? Aren't poise and confidence going to help them handle the loss/failure with good grace—and to be assured that they only need try again?

Alfie Kohn contends competition "is to self-esteem as sugar is to teeth." In *No Contest*, he writes: "The idea that children should be accepted and loved unconditionally—rather than in proportion to the number of others they have beaten at something—is a very peculiar idea to many Americans." But it doesn't have to be this way. And if we want our children to grow up to be self-assured, ethical adults—who also happen to have positive feelings about physical activity—then it really shouldn't be.

Superkids and Specialization

A policy statement issued by the AAP in July 2000 begins: "Children involved in sports should be encouraged to participate in a variety of different activities and develop a wide range of skills. Young athletes who specialize in just one sport may be denied the benefits of varied activity while facing additional physical, physiologic, and psychological demands from intense training and competition."

Why was such a statement necessary? Because more and more children are being persuaded to specialize in a single sport or discipline at earlier and earlier ages. It seems it's not enough to be a superkid in general; a child must excel in just one area. A child must be a *specialist*, in the hopes of attracting awards, honors, a college scholarship, and—who knows?—even an Olympic medal or an invitation from the pros. But the notion of children as specialists is a really bad idea.

One of the best and most important parts of being a kid is having the chance to *dabble*—to explore and experiment. To learn where one's strengths and weaknesses lie—one's likes and dislikes, passions and indifferences. To discover skills in *many* areas, so one is both well rounded and blessed with a wide variety of choices in life. After all, how much sense does it make to focus on a single skill to the exclusion of all others? Not only does that make for a rather boring life (remember the expression "Variety is the spice of life?"), but it can also be disastrous should an injury or burnout occur. Besides, even if an individual were to go all the way to the pros, there are very few competitive sports one can play for an entire lifetime. A person needs to know how to do something else!

In a television interview aired during the 2002 Winter Olympics, figure skater Dorothy Hamill talked about her childhood and her training. Dorothy was one of those children whose family was split apart when she and her mom moved to be closer to her coach. Dorothy's life was centered around her skating; she wasn't required to focus on anything else. As a result she won an Olympic gold medal. But a funny thing happened on the way to the rest of her life: her too-focused existence never prepared her for the real world. Dorothy has since experienced bankruptcy and two divorces.

Was it worth it? Only Dorothy could tell you. But there sure was a lot of sadness in her eyes as she told her story. And many, many professional athletes have said they want a lot more for their own children. Indeed, according to one study, more than half of the successful athletes surveyed said that, if they had a five-year-old child, they would make sure she participated in activities other than sports.

When a child specializes too early, other parts of his personality can remain underdeveloped. As David Elkind points out, this can result in something either as simple as an inability to talk about any other subject or as disturbing as some really strange behavior. Dr. Elkind uses Michael Jackson's plastic surgery and his chimpanzee confidant as an example of the latter. And Ian Tofler and Theresa Foy DiGeronimo emphasize that the majority of precocious children are simply that: ahead of the game at first but not necessarily more gifted over time. They argue that skills develop at different rates in different individuals and often "plateau on equal ground." Moreover, they say, the people who have the most trouble adjusting to disappointment in life are those who characterize themselves by only one quality.

However, even if we don't look at the big picture—at the child's distant future—there are two very good reasons (one physical and one emotional) in the here and now that specialization at an early age should be discouraged.

As the AAP policy statement reveals: "Certain aspects of the growing athlete may predispose the child and adolescent to repetitive stress injuries such as traction apophysitis (Osgood-Schlatter disease; Sever disease; medial epicondylitis [Little League elbow]); injuries to developing joint surfaces (osteochondritis dissecans); and/or injuries to the immature spine (spondylolysis; spondylolisthesis; vertebral apophysitis)." Even if we've never heard such words before—and most of us haven't—it all sounds pretty scary.

In plain English: before a child has reached physical maturity, the extensive use of the same muscle groups and joints can lead to tissue breakdown and injuries. Dr. Lyle Micheli, one of the founders of the country's first pediatric sports medicine clinics, has seen some major changes in the field since opening the clinic at Boston Children's Hospital in 1974. Among them is the fact that pediatric sports medicine has become a burgeoning field. Also, knee injuries like patellar pain syndrome were previously unheard of in children; they're now the number-one diagnosis at his clinic. And phrases like *Little League elbow, swimmer's shoulder*, and *gymnast's back* are commonly tossed about.

According to an ABC news report, in 1990, more than 140,000 children from Dixie League, Little League, and Pony League baseball ended up in hospital emergency rooms. The U.S. Consumer Product Safety Commission reports that more than four million children are treated for sports injuries in emergency rooms each year, with another eight million treated by their family doctors. In a 1990 *Newsweek* piece, Dr. Micheli emphasized that growing children are particularly susceptible to overuse injuries "because of the softness of their growing bones and the relative tightness of their ligaments, tendons, and muscles during growth spurts." He also cautioned that overuse injuries develop slowly and subtly and, as a result, often go undetected. When this happens, the damage can become permanent and bring about such diseases as arthritis in later life.

What are common causes of overuse injuries? Pitching in baseball (the experts recommend children not be allowed to pitch until age eight), the flexion and extension of the back common to gymnastics and some forms of dance, the pounding of the feet against the ground in dance and tennis, as well as the constant jumping and landing in track and field, dance, and gymnastics. Even if your child doesn't participate in one of these activities, intensive training in any sport or physical discipline can result in acute or chronic injury. The AAP warns against children competing at a high level requiring training regimens that can be considered extreme even for adults!

Naturally such training regimens have emotional repercussions as well—in the form of burnout. Although burnout in kids seems a preposterous notion (after all, it wasn't that long ago that most adults were unfamiliar with the term), it's happening with frightening frequency. And, really, should we be surprised? We're turning our children into juvenile workaholics trying to manage impossible schedules. Fred Engh laments the fact that child athletes are afraid to take even brief breaks from their sports, lest they fall behind their peers. And Barbara Carlson, one of the founding members of Putting Family First, an organization dedicated to prioritizing family life, recounts stories of one child being benched because he attended his sister's wedding and another unable to go to his grandmother's house for Thanksgiving dinner because there was practice that afternoon! Where's the balance—or the sanity—in that?

Tofler and DiGeronimo list the following signs of burnout in *Keeping Your Kids Out Front Without Kicking Them from Behind*:

- Moodiness or anger
- Defiance
- Anxiety and stress
- Fatigue and chronic pain
- Insomnia
- Withdrawal
- Deteriorating performance and a feeling that one has "peaked"
- Lack of enjoyment; feeling stale
- Boredom
- Loss of idealism and purpose

Others can include weight loss, chronic injuries or illnesses, loss of self-esteem, and falling behind in school. If a child is experiencing one or more of these symptoms, chances are she's been focusing exclusively on one activity and working way too hard at it.

The experts recommend that children under twelve participate in a variety of activities and sports—not just one. Even better, they say, young children should be allowed to dabble in a number of different areas—but not to the point where they're spinning so many plates overhead that a crash is inevitable.

There are two important points to keep in mind here. First, if physical activity causes the burnout, the child is more than likely to avoid physical activity in the future. Second, burnout doesn't touch only one area of an individual's life; it affects his whole life, as anyone who has ever experienced it can tell you.

We would never insist a mathematically gifted child study nothing but math in school. Likewise, we shouldn't expect a child with a special sports skill to give up everything else in her life. Children—and their interests—change almost daily. They should be allowed the childhood privilege of trying and rejecting a great number of interests at least until commitment is a concept they can fully understand and appreciate.

Sure, we've all heard the stories about Tiger Woods taking up golf with a miniclub at the age of one and Sarah Hughes, 2002 Olympic figure skating champion, proclaiming on video at age five that she wanted to win the gold medal. But they are rare exceptions to the rule! When sixty-three of the world's greatest athletes were interviewed by Olympic hurdler and author David Hemery, only five of them reported specializing in just one sport before the age of twelve. And the more important fact? According to a survey conducted by *USA Today* and NBC, a whopping 75 percent of the children who'd started playing organized sports at six or seven had stopped playing by age fifteen. Childhood is a special time. It's a time to be loved unconditionally—for *everything* you are and not just one skill you may possess. As parents it's not our job to raise a baseball player or a black belt in karate. It's our job to raise well-rounded individuals who can make great choices in life.

Some Sports Stats

- The average child/adolescent spends eleven hours a week participating in her or his sport.
- Of the Canadian youth hockey players who'd learned violent and illegal tactics by watching and playing hockey, over 60 percent said they'd used the tactics themselves.
- Only 25 percent of the stars of youth leagues become stars in high school.
- Fewer than 1 percent of children playing organized sports will obtain a college athletic scholarship.
- Of the two million gymnasts competing each year, only seven or eight will participate in the Olympics every *four years*.
- The odds of a high school football player getting to the pros are six thousand to one.
- The odds of a high school basketball player getting to the pros are ten thousand to one.

3

The Good News
About Physical Activity

"If anything is sacred, the human body is sacred."

—WALT WHITMAN

CALL IT *physical activity*. Call it *movement*. Call it *active* or *physical play*. Heck, call it *exercise*. (One colleague argues that if we call it exercise when children are physically active and enjoying it, the word won't have any negative connotations when the children become adults.) Whatever we call it, there are plenty of excellent reasons that children should be engaging in it.

Professionals in relevant fields, of course, would balk at the idea of using these terms interchangeably, as they have very specific definitions for each of them. Physical activity, they say, is any movement produced by skeletal muscles, resulting in the expenditure of energy. Some simply refer to it as the state of not being sedentary or asleep. Exercise, on the other hand, is considered a subcategory of physical activity and usually refers to movement that is structured, repetitive, and used specifically for the purpose of attaining fitness (think sit-ups and jumping jacks). While play may or may not produce meaningful energy expenditure (playing with blocks, for example, will not), most active or physical play (running, jumping, swinging, and climbing) will.

For our purposes, though, it's all about children moving. All of the preceding terms will be used throughout this chapter to describe any time infants and young children are moving—whether it's movement that burns calories, like galloping and dancing (counteracting the effects of sedentary behavior described in Chapter 1) or movement that promotes motor development or learning (walking across a balance beam or playing peek-aboo, respectively). However, these words and phrases will *not* refer to the hyperorganized, adult-directed kind of movement too often experienced by "superkids." Rather, the physical activity described in this chapter will signify movement and play that are developmentally appropriate for and come naturally to children—whether they're of the unstructured (child-directed) or structured (planned and perhaps facilitated by adults) variety.

Although we may think of movement only in terms of what it provides physically (and there's plenty of that), in actuality movement makes major contributions to the development of the whole child: physically, socially, emotionally, and cognitively. In other words, it can help make your child healthier, better skilled, better adjusted, and even smarter. We're talking about an inexpensive, simple, couldn't-be-more-natural means of giving your child the best life has to offer.

Skeptical? Then read on.

Let's Get Physical

Since movement is most often associated with physical results, let's begin there. According to a report of the U.S. surgeon general, although the benefits of physical activity have been proclaimed throughout Western history, scientific evidence to back up the claims emerged only during the second half of the twentieth century. We now have a growing understanding of how physical activity affects the musculoskeletal, cardiovascular, respiratory, and endocrine systems. More specifically, the report indicates that regular physical activity benefits health in the following ways:

- Reduces the risk of dying prematurely (sedentary adults have twice the mortality rate of those who are at least somewhat active)

- Reduces the risk of dying from heart disease
- Reduces the risk of developing diabetes
- Helps reduce blood pressure in people who already have high blood pressure
- Reduces the risk of developing colon cancer
- Reduces feelings of depression and anxiety
- Helps control weight
- Increases the body's infection-fighting white blood cells and germ-fighting antibodies
- Helps build and maintain healthy bones, muscles, and joints

Sounds good. If this were all of what physical activity had to offer, there'd be reason enough to partake in it. (Surely a daily tablet offering similar benefits would sell by the billions.) But there's even more.

Although most of the research has been conducted on the relationship between physical activity and adult health, there's now enough evidence to show physical activity causes health benefits for children and adolescents as well. Improved aerobic endurance, muscle growth, muscular strength, motor coordination, and growth stimulation of the heart, lungs, and other vital organs are among these benefits. Research in Canada has even discovered that the most active young people are the least likely to smoke! And while physical activity is important for healthy children, it has added benefit for those with chronic disease risk factors. The CDC states that it decreases blood pressure in those with borderline hypertension and both increases fitness and decreases the degree of overweight in obese children.

Considering the rising rate of obesity among children and its related health and emotional risks, as reported in Chapter 1, the latter point seems reason enough to get our children moving! But there's even more. The surgeon general's report contends that weight-bearing physical activity (walking, running, and skipping, for example) is essential for normal development during childhood and adolescence.

Why? Partly because it is during childhood and adolescence that a person's bones experience the most growth. As such, researchers have found that exercise before puberty offers the maximum benefits with regard to bone density and strength. Exercise begun after puberty tends to result in only small increases in bone density. And when children miss out on the opportunity to create bone mass, osteoporosis (especially among females) may be the eventual result.

The bad news here is that, according to a University of Iowa study that looked at 368 children between the ages of four and six, children are not active enough to promote optimal bone health. And, unfortunately, the girls were less active than the boys. The good news is that it doesn't take a lot to turn the situation around. Here, again, weight-bearing movement is the most valuable. Though it should be vigorous, it doesn't have to be sustained for long periods. Kathleen Janz, lead author of the study, recommends ten to fifteen minutes a day. We can help our children accomplish this simply by insisting they spend some time outdoors each day!

It is also in the outdoors that children are most likely to participate in the vigorous activity that brings necessary oxygen to the muscles, contributes to cardiovascular health, and increases the number of capillaries in the brain, resulting in greater absorption of nutrients and elimination of waste products. Play specialist Eric Strickland extols the virtues of such outdoor activities as climbing, swinging, and sliding. Sure, the children look like they're just having fun; but there's plenty more going on. Writing in *Scholastic Early Childhood Today*, Strickland maintains that swinging helps children develop coordination, and sliding, which stimulates the ear canal and its fluids, helps promote a sense of balance. As for climbing, he states:

- Reaching for rungs above the shoulder raises the arms, thereby increasing the cardiovascular flow.
- Stretching increases and maintains flexibility.
- Pulling up with hands and arms while climbing a ladder builds upper body, grip, and arm strength.
- Climbing steps and ladders develops leg strength and coordination.

Climbing up and down slides also requires planning and problem-solving skills for very young children. And climbing back down the slide's ladder requires even greater balance to prevent falling.

As mentioned, most of the research on the relationship between physical activity and good health has been conducted with adults. However, there are two corresponding points to keep in mind where children are concerned: there's evidence showing that individuals who are active as children are more likely to be active as adults. There's also evidence determining that *in*activity tracks from childhood into adulthood.

It only makes sense, therefore, that we get kids turned on to physical activity while they're young so they'll continue to move as they grow older. That way they can derive positive health benefits both as children and as adults.

Kids as Competent Movers

If all of these health-related benefits aren't motive enough to make sure your child gets and stays active, there's yet another good reason—also in the physical domain—for young children to move: it helps develop movement skills.

Like other skills acquired in the early years, movement skills need to be taught and practiced if they're to be mastered. Although it seems motor skills miraculously appear and develop on their own, the fact is, children who don't receive instruction and practice in this area will develop only marginal—as opposed to maximal—ability to use their bodies.

It only makes sense. Just as children acquire a vocabulary of words to use throughout life, they likewise acquire and develop a "movement vocabulary" consisting of fundamental locomotor (traveling), nonlocomotor (stationary), and manipulative (object-control) skills they can use for current and future physical activity. And just as we would never expect a child's language development to mature without help from us and without practice talking—and talking and talking—we can't expect movement skills to mature fully without assistance and without their moving . . . and moving and moving.

Then there's the theory of "critical periods" or "windows of opportunity." Although their existence has been suspected for some time, critical periods have been receiving more scientific support of late. The theory contends that nature provides certain times when the child's experience can have the greatest impact on various aspects of her development. These "windows of opportunity" begin opening before birth but shrink as the child gets older. For basic motor skills the critical period—the time during which experience can have the most influence—seems to extend from the prenatal stage to about age five.

Does this mean that a child who doesn't take full advantage of this critical period will be damaged for life? No. But it can mean that, without enough appropriate movement experience from birth to five, the child will miss out on the opportunity to achieve the best possible motor skill development. And the experts feel that, for certain skills, there is definitely a "too late." The brain's motor neurons must be trained between the ages of two and eleven, or they won't be "plastic" enough to be rewired later in life.

Of course not every child will go on to play sports, compete in gymnastics, or study dance. For those who don't, optimal motor skill development wouldn't seem to be such a big deal. But it is the individual who feels competent and confident when moving who will most likely continue moving throughout life—who will most likely take part in lifelong physical activity and thereby achieve all of the health benefits it has to offer. Adolescents and adults who haven't acquired and mastered fundamental movement skills are the ones who shy away from physical activity because the movements required feel unnatural and overly strenuous; learning them at an older age is much more challenging. And the fear of failing and looking foolish is a powerful deterrent. (Have you ever witnessed someone refusing to get on the dance floor with his partner or freezing at her turn to serve in a family volleyball game?)

Moreover, research has found that children without the ability to execute basic motor skills are three times more sedentary than skilled children! And, because children judge themselves—and others—by their movement ability, children who move well simply have a better view of themselves overall.

Naturally, those children who do go on to take part in sports, dance, or other physical activities requiring more complex skills will have an added advantage—because mastering basic skills is essential to mastering later, more difficult movements. Not only will their confidence in their movement abilities lead them to take on greater physical challenges, but also it will keep them participating. Children and adolescents who drop out of sports think less of their abilities than those who stick with it. Most likely the same can be said of those who withdraw from other physical experiences, like dancing or aerobics, as well.

Moving Toward Well-Adjusted, Sociable Children

It's easy to see the role of movement in physical development. Movement's role in your child's social/emotional development may be a bit more challenging to envision. But that doesn't mean it's nonexistent. On the contrary, physical activity and play have plenty to do with how children develop socially and emotionally.

Here's just some of what the research tells us:

- Physical activity is consistently associated with higher levels of self-esteem (the value the child places on herself) and self-concept (the understanding the child has of herself).
- Because they offer young children independence, muscle control and good eye-hand coordination enhance children's feelings of effectiveness.
- Physical activity contributes to better body image and mood and to an overall improved sense of well-being.
- Physical activity improves self-confidence.
- Physical activity can have a positive impact on moral reasoning.
- Physically skilled children tend to be more popular with their peers, even among preschoolers.

Any one of these benefits would be something we'd want to give our children. But it's especially important here to pause and differentiate between developmentally appropriate movement (whether structured, as in physical education, or unstructured, as at recess or in the backyard) and organized sport. The *former* offers the benefits just listed. The latter, as mentioned in the last chapter, barely even offers physical activity—let alone the benefits that can be derived from it.

When children organize their *own* games, they learn much in the social/emotional domain. Laying down the ground rules helps children understand the necessity for rules. Reworking the rules as needed helps children acquire flexibility in their thinking, develop problem-solving skills, and take the perspective of others (an absolutely vital social skill). Children who make up and organize their own games learn to avoid conflict—and, when it can't be avoided, to resolve it. In fact play experts contend that, when adults step in too soon, they may unwittingly be preventing children from learning to work things out. Some play researchers maintain that children provided chances to develop strong conflict resolution skills in the early years may become involved in fewer violent conflicts later in life.

Child-organized games also afford opportunities for participants to practice leadership skills and self-discipline. This lends itself to positive self-esteem, which some contend is necessary for the development of trust in human relationships. Further, children engaged in self-directed play gain a sense of autonomy (self-sufficiency) and learn to share, take turns, and develop impulse control. They're not afraid to take creative risks or to make a mistake because, in true play, there's no such thing as failure. Mistakes made are simply corrected. Although the children may not always get their way, this, too, teaches an important lesson.

Even rough-and-tumble play, predominant among boys, has valuable lessons to teach. Writing in the journal *Child Development*, David J. Bjork-lund and Rhonda Douglas Brown state, "The greatest impact of rough-and-tumble play . . . is in the social domain, facilitating . . . the encoding and decoding of social signals." And, for girls, physical play in the outdoors teaches them to be more assertive than does pretend play indoors.

Then there's the matter of stress and anxiety, which fall into both the social/emotional and physical domains. Physical activity reduces levels of stress and anxiety by impacting both areas.

From an emotional point of view, play allows children to work out and deal with their fears and anxieties. Physiologically speaking, play specialist Scott Liebler explains that movements involving the whole body help release muscular contractions, allowing the body's natural energies to circulate freely. This, in turn, puts the brain in a more relaxed state. Says Eric Jensen, author of *Arts with the Brain in Mind*, "Gross motor movements . . . increase dopamine production, one of the brain's reward chemicals." In addition, exercise regulates serotonin, the body's "mood stabilizer."

Though stress and anxiety are typically associated with adulthood, we need to realize that many of today's children are experiencing them in unhealthy levels. Being obese is stressful. Being a superkid is stressful. Trying to live up to the expectations—particularly the unrealistic ones—of the important adults in their lives is very stressful to young children. With too much stress and anxiety the eventual result can be high blood pressure or heart disease. Stress and anxiety can also lead to depression, alcohol or drug abuse, and poor interpersonal relationships. Physical activity—the nonstressful, noncompetitive kind—can help children unwind.

When Kids Cooperate

Learning to cooperate with others is a social skill and has emotional consequences. But because society places more and more value on competition—at younger and younger ages—and because cooperation has so very much to offer on its own, it's being granted a separate section here.

Used here, the term *cooperation* is not intended to refer to good behavior or compliance. Rather, it means the positive collaboration that takes place between and among children—as seen, for example, when children devise their own games, alternate turning the jump rope for one another, and play cooperative musical chairs (described later).

Unlike competition, which research shows can foster antisocial behaviors, cooperation has been determined to promote *pro*social behaviors. Steve Grineski, author of *Cooperative Learning in Physical Education*, says the social skills needed for cooperative learning include:

- Listening to others
- Resolving conflict
- Supporting and encouraging others
- Taking turns
- Expressing enjoyment in the success of others
- Demonstrating the ability to criticize ideas, not individuals

In *No Contest*, Alfie Kohn identifies a great deal of research demonstrating cooperation's positive effects on both social and emotional development. Kohn says cooperation:

A Special Story About Cooperation

A while back a story began circulating via E-mail. It went like this:

> A few years ago, at the Seattle Special Olympics, nine contestants, all physi-
> cally or mentally disabled, assembled at the starting line for the hundred-yard
> dash. At the gun they all started out—not exactly in a dash, but with a relish
> to run the race to the finish and win. All, that is, except one little boy, who
> stumbled on the asphalt, tumbled over a couple of times, and began to cry.
>
> The other eight heard the boy cry. They slowed down and looked back.
> Then they all turned around and went back—every one of them.
>
> One girl with Down's syndrome bent down and kissed him and said, "This
> will make it better." Then all nine linked arms and walked together to the fin-
> ish line. Everyone in the stadium stood, and the cheering went on for several
> minutes.
>
> People who were there are still telling the story. Why? Because deep
> down we know this one thing: what matters in this life is more than winning
> for ourselves. What matters in this life is helping others win, even if it means
> slowing down and changing our course.

According to information at snopes.com, the story, as written, is actually an
"urban legend." The true story is that, in 1976, at a Special Olympics event in
Spokane, one participant did take a fall; and one or two other racers did turn back.
But it was only two or three participants who crossed the finish line together—not
all of them.

Why, then, did the E-mail version of the story take on a life of its own? Who
knows how these stories get started and then transform? But two things seem evident: the original story touched people's hearts and so was passed on. And the story
was eventually adapted to serve as an example of how we would *like* things to be.

The Latin roots of the word *competition* are *com* (together) and *peter* (to
strive). *Striving together.* It seems that idea is more of a human imperative than
winning at all costs.

- Is more conducive to psychological health
- Leads to friendlier feelings among participants
- Promotes a feeling of being in control of one's life
- Increases self-esteem
- Results in greater sensitivity and trust toward others
- Enhances feelings of belonging
- Increases motivation

When children are given the chance to work together toward a solution or common goal—whether creating a game or building a human pyramid—they know they each contribute to the success of the venture. Each child realizes he or she plays a vital role in the outcome, and each accepts the responsibility of fulfilling that role. They also learn to become tolerant of others' ideas and to accept the similarities and differences of other children. Furthermore, cooperative activities seldom cause the feelings of inferiority that can result from the comparisons made during competition. On the contrary, because cooperative and noncompetitive activities lead to a greater chance for success, they generate greater confidence in children.

Although competition is commonly believed to be human nature, Scott Scheer, an associate professor in the Department of Human and Community Resource Development at The Ohio State University, contends we humans actually have a "cooperative imperative"—a desire to work with others toward mutual goals that can run the spectrum from conceiving a child to sending a rocket to the moon. He may be right. Using MRI technology to determine the effects of both competition and cooperation, scientists at Emory University recently found that when people collaborate, the brain sends out pleasure responses.

Terry Orlick, a professor at the University of Ottawa, has long been a proponent of cooperative games. As he says in *The Second Cooperative Sports & Games Book*, games can be "a beautiful way to bring people together. However, if you distort children's play by rewarding excessive competition, physical aggression against others, cheating, and unfair play, you distort children's lives."

On the other hand, about cooperative games, he says the concept is simple: "People play with one another rather than against one another; they play to overcome challenges, not to overcome other people; and they are freed by the very structure of the games to enjoy the play experience itself. No player need find himself or herself a bench warmer nursing a bruised self-image. Since the games are designed so that cooperation among players is necessary to achieve the objective(s) of the game, children play together for common ends rather than against one another for mutually exclusive ends. In the process, they learn in a fun way how to become more considerate of one another, more aware of how other people are feeling, and more willing to operate in one another's best interests."

Traditional competitive games are often easily modified to be cooperative. Think back to the last chapter and the image of traditional musical chairs. When the possibility exists for only one winner and many losers, the situation can get ugly. Children will do whatever it takes to keep from being eliminated and labeled a loser! But with a simple modification, you have cooperative musical chairs, in which chairs are still removed with every round—again until there's only one left. But the goal is for all of the children to find a way to *share* the remaining chairs—even when just one remains.

The results are hilarious. Instead of punching, poking, kicking, scratching, and screaming, the children are laughing and giggling. You can practically watch their brains working as they try to solve the increasingly challenging problem! And when the game is over and they've achieved a solution (possibilities include everything from lap sitting, to one child sitting and the others creating a chain by holding hands, to every child placing just his or her toes on the chair), they're all winners. And they feel great! Moreover, they've learned valuable lessons about working with others and solving problems.

It's no wonder the research shows preschoolers prefer cooperative activities to competitive ones. It's no wonder the research shows cooperative activities have far more to offer children than competitive ones.

More Movement, Smarter Kids

OK. So you can see how physical activity can impact not only your child's physical development but also his social/emotional development. But intel-

Let's Cooperate!

What's an alternative to competitive games and activities? *Cooperative* games and activities! In addition to the social/emotional benefits offered, all of the following games have physical and cognitive components as well. They also help develop pre-sports skills. For example, they all promote teamwork. And they foster body and spatial awareness, which, among other things, prepares children to know where they are in relation to an object—like a ball or an opponent or a teammate. Finally, the problem solving that is part of many of these games is a handy skill to have in all areas of life.

Following are partner activities for you and your child, for your children to play together, or for your child to play with a friend. Of course, you can always use them with groups of children, as long as there is an even number of participants.

Mirror Game

Partners stand facing each other. One partner performs a series of simple movements in slow motion (standing in place), which the second partner mirrors. After a while partners reverse roles. The object is not to try to trick each other but to resemble a mirror reflection as closely as possible.

Shadow Game

This is similar to the previous activity, but one partner stands with her or his back to the second partner and performs various *traveling* movements around the room that the latter "shadows." Again, partners eventually reverse roles, so both have a chance to lead and follow.

Lightning and Thunder

The partners decide who is first going to be lightning and who is first going to be thunder. When ready, the partners separate and begin moving about the room, keeping their eyes on one another. The partner acting as lightning will periodically "strike" (move like lightning). And, since thunder is the sound that follows lightning, the partner acting as thunder will then respond by moving in a way he or she feels depicts thunder. After a while, partners reverse roles.

It Takes Two

This activity requires partners to connect various body parts (matching parts, like right hands, left elbows, or right feet; or nonmatching parts, like a hand and an elbow, an elbow and a shoulder, or a wrist and a hip). There are two objects to the game: to stay connected and to see how many ways it's possible to move while remaining connected.

Palm to Palm

Partners face each other, close enough to touch. The first assumes a shape with her or his arms (any shape is OK as long as palms face the partner). The partner then forms the identical shape, bringing hands palm to palm with those of the first child. As soon as contact is made, the first partner chooses a new arm position, and the activity proceeds. After a while, partners reverse roles.

Footsie Rolls

This is a challenging game that requires some space but is lots of fun. Partners lie on their backs with the soles of their feet together. They then must see how far they can roll without their feet breaking contact!

Here are some cooperative games for when *groups* of children get together.

Switcheroo

Partners stand back to back. You then call out the name of a body part or parts (for example, "hands" or "knees"). The children then turn, bring together the body parts called out, and then immediately get back to back again. When you call out "switcheroo," the children find new partners and the process starts again. To add a bit more challenge to the activity, call out nonmatching parts, too (for example, "hand to knee").

Pass a Face

The children sit in a circle, and one child begins by making a face that is "passed" to the child to her right or left. That child makes the *same* face and passes it along in the same direction. When the face has been passed all around the circle, the process is repeated, with a different child beginning and a different face.

Pass a Movement

This is similar to the preceding game, but the children form a standing circle and pass an *action*. The first child might, for instance, bend at the waist and straighten. Each child in succession must then do the same.

Pass a Beat

The first child claps out a rhythm (e.g., one-two-three at a moderate tempo). The object is for each child in the circle to repeat the rhythm *exactly*, keeping an even tempo all the way around. Even the interval between children should be in keeping with the rhythm being passed.

Group Balance

The children form a standing circle and place their hands on the shoulders of the children beside them. They must then maintain a steady balance through challenges to stand on only one foot; lean forward, backward, left, and right; rise onto tiptoes; and so on.

This Is My Friend

The children stand in a circle holding hands, and one child raises the arm of the child to his right or left, saying, "This is my friend. . . ." The child whose arm has been raised announces her name and then raises the arm of the next child in the circle, saying, "This is my friend. . . ." The process continues all the way around the circle, with arms remaining raised until the last child has had a chance to say his name. When that happens, the children take a deep bow for a job well done.

A variation of this game, if all the children know one another, is for them to introduce each other. In other words, one child raises the arm of the child to her right or left and says, "This is my friend [Michael]."

---

lectual development? What could movement possibly have to do with learning? After all, schools—where most of the child's learning is supposed to take place—are our prime promoters of *inactivity*. ("Sit still." "Stop squirming." "Don't run." "Stay in your seat.") If movement were critical to learning, wouldn't the schools be employing it?

Certainly, you'd think so. Those of us who've understood the connection between moving and learning for a very long time have been waiting just as long for the educational "revolution." And yet not only is movement in the classroom a rarity, but also physical education and recess are being eliminated as though they were completely irrelevant to children's growth and development. Perhaps the revolution will finally arrive only when you, as a parent, become aware of movement's role in cognitive development and learning and begin to insist the schools do what's right for children and not merely what's convenient.

But let's begin with infancy, when it's probably easier to believe in the connection between moving and learning. After all, you can literally *see* the baby's motor development and the learning that results. First she merely follows an object with her eyes. Then she learns to reach for and eventually grasp the object. At about six months she'll throw the object over and over again. Although it seems she takes some perverse pleasure in seeing you retrieve, she's actually learning an important lesson in cause and effect. And from one stage to the next she discovers how to make the adjustments necessary to accomplish these tasks. (As she does all this, connections among brain cells develop and strengthen. You'll find more on this in the next chapter.)

Also, as your baby moves from a lying to a sitting to a creeping and, finally, to a standing position, his perspective changes. As his body position shifts, so does his perception of the world. And, as he becomes more mobile, he's able to continually increase his knowledge about himself and the people and things around him. Because he's not yet visually oriented, he primarily uses his other senses—particularly his tactile (touch), kinesthetic (muscular), and proprioceptive (body awareness) senses—to acquire the greatest amount of information.

As Einstein so succinctly pointed out, "Learning is experience. Everything else is just information." And so it goes for the first two years of life, as the child learns through trial and error: experiments, discovers, experiences, and understands. Piaget, the noted child development specialist studied by future teachers, labeled this learning *sensorimotor* and determined it was the child's earliest form of learning. Since then, brain research has proven him right.

But the most recent brain research has done much more than that. It's now understood that, because a child's earliest learning is based on motor development, so is much of the knowledge that follows. The cerebellum, the part of the brain previously associated with motor control only, is now known to be, as Eric Jensen, author of numerous books on brain-based learning, puts it, a "virtual switchboard of cognitive activity." Study after study has demonstrated a connection between the cerebellum and such cognitive functions as memory, spatial orientation, attention, language, and decision making, among others.

Thanks to advances in brain research, we now know that most of the brain is activated during physical activity—much more so than when doing seat work. In fact, according to Jensen, sitting for more than ten minutes at a stretch "reduces our awareness of physical and emotional sensations and increases fatigue." He tells us this results in reduced concentration and, in children, most likely discipline problems.

Movement, on the other hand, increases the capacity of blood vessels (and possibly even their number), allowing for the delivery of oxygen, water, and glucose ("brain food") to the brain. And this can't help optimizing the brain's performance!

All of this, of course, contradicts the longstanding and much-loved belief that children learn best when they're sitting still and listening and working quietly at their desks. It also helps us understand why:

- One Canadian study showed academic scores went up when a third of the school day was devoted to physical education.
- Another Canadian study demonstrated children participating in five hours of vigorous physical activity a week had stronger academic performance in math, English, natural sciences, and French than did children with only two hours of physical activity per week.
- A study of third-grade children participating in dance activities improved their reading skills by 13 percent over six months, while their peers, who were sedentary, showed a decrease of 2 percent.
- In France, children who spent eight hours a week in physical education demonstrated better academic performance, greater independence, and more maturity than students with only forty minutes of PE a week.
- Children who participate in daily physical education have been shown to perform better academically and to have a better attitude toward school.
- A study conducted by neurophysiologist Carla Hannaford determined that children who spent an extra hour a day exercising did better on exams than students who didn't exercise.

- Recent research demonstrates a direct link between fitness and intelligence, particularly in children under sixteen and in the elderly.

It is a huge mistake to think the mind and body are separate entities. George Graham, in his book *Teaching Children Physical Education*, points out the sheer silliness of this long-held belief with an anecdote concerning his arguments to school boards determined to eliminate physical education. He tells them life would be simpler—and certainly more cost-effective—if we could simply bus the children's heads to school. But, unfortunately, their heads happen to be attached to bodies! The book then shows a cartoon of headless children walking into the gym. The point? We're teaching only minds in the classroom and only bodies in the gymnasium. But it's not supposed to be that way!

The truth is that the domains of child development—physical, social, emotional, and cognitive—simply do not mature separately from one another. There's an overlap and interrelatedness among them. And children do not differentiate among thinking, feeling, and moving. Thus, when a child learns something related to one domain, it impacts the others.

For young children especially, involving multiple senses in the learning process is a must—which makes it ideal that there's a strong connection between many of the concepts found in physical education and those concepts children must learn in other content areas. For example, such concepts as spatial relationships, line, and shape are related to both physical education and the content areas of math and art. Direction and rhythm are just two of the concepts physical education and language arts have in common. The discovery of the capabilities and limitations of the body and body parts falls under the heading of science for young children. And learning to interact with partners and as part of a group is directly related to social studies in early childhood.

It's no wonder research shows that movement is young children's preferred mode of learning—because they best *understand* concepts that are experienced physically. For example, children need to get into high and low, small and large, wide and narrow body shapes to truly understand these quantitative concepts. They need to act out simple computation problems

More Than One Kind of Intelligence

In 1983 developmental psychologist Howard Gardner of Harvard University wrote a groundbreaking book called *Frames of Mind: The Theory of Multiple Intelligences*. In it he demonstrated that intelligence isn't a singular entity that can be tested only with paper and pencil. Instead, using specific, scientific criteria, he determined we each possess several kinds of intelligence, to varying degrees, and in different combinations. Twenty years later this work is still making an impact in the world of education.

Originally Gardner identified seven "kinds of smart"—that is, seven different ways that children (all individuals, really) have of learning and knowing. Among them was the bodily/kinesthetic intelligence, which is strong in people who solve problems or who create with their bodies or body parts. This, of course, includes athletes like Michael Jordan and dancers like Martha Graham. But it also includes craftspeople, surgeons, and even chefs like Julia Child and Emeril Lagasse, who rely on their hands in their work.

Among the other intelligences Gardner has identified are linguistic (people who are "word smart"), logical/mathematical (those with strong reasoning/"number smart" skills), spatial (those who can envision how things orient in space), interpersonal (people who relate well to others), intrapersonal (those who know themselves well), and musical (people interested in sounds and the patterns they can create). Respectively, people strong in these intelligences often become writers and speakers; scientists, engineers, and mathematicians; navigators, architects, and artists; counselors and teachers; entrepreneurs; and musicians and composers. Surgeons would likely be most developed in not only the bodily/kinesthetic but also the logical/mathematical intelligence.

Gardner's point—so seized upon by educators—is that no one kind of intelligence is better than another. (It's not how smart you are; it's *how* you are smart.) Although the linguistic and logical/mathematical intelligences are the most validated in our society—and are the basis for all standardized and IQ tests—people strong in these two areas are no more intelligent than someone whose strengths lie in, say, the musical and bodily/kinesthetic intelligences. Teachers who've studied the multiple intelligences now know that, should a child have difficulty solving a math problem in the traditional way, he just might need to act it out, manipulate some objects, or make up a song about it. The important thing is not how he got it but that he did get it!

All young children rely heavily on their bodily/kinesthetic intelligence, and it's up to us not to invalidate this. Besides, when a child is moving, she's not only using and further developing her bodily/kinesthetic intelligence; she's also further developing spatial intelligence. When a child moves in response to musical elements like tempo, volume, rhythm, and pitch, she's enhancing her musical intelligence. When children work together, they're promoting the interpersonal intelligence. And if they're solving movement problems, the logical/mathematical intelligence is involved, too.

The moral of the story? Let the kids move! The theory of multiple intelligences gives us one more argument that more movement makes smarter kids.

(demonstrating the nursery rhyme "Three Little Monkeys" to discover three minus one equals two) to comprehend subtraction. They need to move in slow motion to Bach's "Air on the G String" and rapidly to Rimsky-Korsakov's "Flight of the Bumblebee" to learn the direct relationship between the movement element of time and the musical element of tempo—and to understand the abstract ideas of slow and fast. They have to take on the straight and curving lines of the letters of the alphabet to fully grasp the way in which the letters should be printed.

Writing in *Early Childhood Exchange*, a publication for early childhood professionals, developmental and environmental psychologist Anita Rui Olds says:

> Until children have experiences orienting their bodies in space by going up, on, under, beside, inside, and in front of things, it is possible they will have difficulty dealing with letter identification and the orientation of symbols on a page. The only difference between a small "b" and a small "d," for example, both of which are composed of a line and a circle, depends upon orientation, i.e., which side of the circle is the line on?

Bette Fauth, in a chapter appearing in *Moving and Learning for the Young Child*, contends that the more senses used in the learning process, the more information we hold on to. She tells us we retain:

- 10 percent of what we read
- 20 percent of what we hear
- 30 percent of what we see
- 50 percent of what we hear and see at the same time
- 70 percent of what wc hear, see, and say
- 90 percent of what we hear, see, say, and do

Eric Jensen labels this kind of hands-on learning *implicit*—like learning to ride a bike. At the opposite end of the spectrum is *explicit* learning—like being told the capital of Peru. He asks, if you hadn't ridden a bike in five years, would you still be able to do it? And if you hadn't heard the capital of Peru for five years, would you still remember what it was? Extrinsic learning may be quicker than learning through exploration and discovery, but the latter has greater meaning for children and stays with them longer. There are plenty of reasons for this, but one of them just may be that intrinsic learning creates more neural networks in the brain. And it's more fun!

Carla Hannaford, in *Smart Moves: Why Learning Is Not All in Your Head*, states, "We have spent years and resources struggling to teach people to learn, and yet the standardized achievement test scores go down and illiteracy rises. Could it be that one of the key elements we've been missing is simply movement?"

Physical Activity and Girls

While most of what's been written in this chapter is certainly applicable to both girls and boys, there are some gender differences we should explore here—some issues you need to be aware of if you're going to ensure your daughter gets just as much benefit from physical activity as your son.

Sadly, the history of female participation in physical activity is a great deal shorter than that of males. Historically speaking, it wasn't all that long ago that many physical activities were considered too strenuous or unladylike for young girls and women, who were warned against being tomboys and the possibility of sterility. Although there were some bright spots along the way, it wasn't until the passage of Title IX (of the Education Amendments of 1972) that girls were given greater opportunities to play high school and college sports. And, thankfully, the fitness boom of the 1970s and '80s was particularly attractive to females.

Still, the research shows that girls are less active than boys (they're most inactive between the ages of fourteen and sixteen) and that teenage girls are dropping out of sports at even higher rates than are teenage boys.

The reasons are many and complicated—and some of them actually begin at birth, with parents' expectations for each gender. For example, one study showed that parents—especially fathers—described girls as "softer, finer-featured, smaller, weaker, and more delicate" than boys. Other studies, in which infants were "disguised" in cross-gender clothing, demonstrated that parents brought trucks to the supposed boy babies and dolls to those they considered girls.

As children get older, parents tend to talk more to their daughters, encourage them to help others, and discourage autonomy. Boys, on the other hand, are encouraged to be fearless. One study used videotapes of children on a playground to prove this. The tapes showed that mothers of daughters were more likely to see danger in their activity, and they intervened more quickly and more often than did mothers of sons. Mothers of daughters also issued more statements of caution, while mothers of sons offered more words encouraging risk taking. Similarly, one researcher points out that, when a baby boy falls down, parents make light of it, encouraging the child to get up and try again. On the other hand, when a baby girl takes a tumble, we race over to pick her up and make sure she's OK.

Throughout childhood boys tend to have more interaction with their fathers than girls, with vigorous physical activity predominant in that interaction. Boys also receive more encouragement from both parents and society to participate in physical activity—a message girls are receiving, even if only subconsciously.

Of course parents aren't the only ones in our society promoting gender stereotyping and inequality. Children are bombarded daily with television images marketing what they conceive to be the "norm": boys playing with cars, trucks, and action figures and girls playing with dolls. "Pink" aisles in the toy stores feature dolls, makeup, and miniature appliances, while "blue" aisles offer vehicles and war toys. "Boys'" toys tend to promote problem solving and exploration, which in turn help develop confidence and competence. "Girls'" toys, by contrast, limit exploration and discourage independence and problem solving.

One result of this media pressure is that, regardless of what they may have asked for, boys more often receive activity-oriented toys and games, while girls are given stuffed animals, toy houses, kitchen sets, and dress-up outfits. Researchers have found that no matter what toys are on the children's lists, parents and others give them gender-specific toys. Girls are then praised for playing with dolls—and boys are ignored when displaying nurturing behavior. Girls are also more often praised for how they look, while boys are praised for what they do.

Unfortunately, it doesn't take long for young children to catch on. Children as young as four have said that playing with dolls, picking flowers, dressing up, skipping, and dancing are what girls do. (At least the skipping and dancing are physical activities!) Boys are supposed to be fighting and playing football, baseball, basketball, hockey, soccer, and karate. And, when coaches and peers clearly communicate that activities such as T-ball are a male domain (and they do), the message is heard loud and clear.

Sure, there are differences between the genders. The idea is not to make girls and boys the same—simply to be sure they're afforded equal opportunities and advantages. And sometimes we can do that by knowing how girls and boys *are* different.

For example, many girls are less inclined toward competitive activities. Competition negatively affects their self-concept and even their motor skill development. A large study of culturally, racially, and socioeconomically diverse preschoolers found that the girls preferred to cooperate when learning basic motor skills, while the boys adopted competitive, individualistic methods. So, when physical education classes and other physical activities are dominated by competition, girls are often turned off.

Girls are also less intrinsically motivated than boys to participate in physical activity, and they rely more heavily on adult approval. That means they tend to play it safe by sticking to previously mastered skills that increase their odds of being praised (no risk taking!). It also means that, without encouragement from the important adults in their lives, girls are likely to lose any enthusiasm they may have had for physical activity.

The time has come for things to change. Our girls need movement, too—in certain ways, even more than our boys do. Because osteoporosis is more prevalent among women, it's especially important for girls to build strong bones when they're young. Exercise has been shown to increase strength in girls significantly. And estrogen-dependent cancers (breast, ovarian, and endometrial) may occur less often in women who exercise.

Depression, too, which is experienced twice as often by adolescent females as by adolescent males, can be impacted positively by exercise. According to a report of the President's Council on Physical Fitness and Sports, entitled "Physical Activity and Sport in the Lives of Girls," participation in physical activity helps counteract the feelings of hopelessness and worthlessness common to depression and helps instill feelings of success. Self-esteem, self-concept, and body image—all of which girls struggle with—are also affected positively by physical activity and exercise. Two recent studies even demonstrated that the more adolescent females participated in physical activity, the more likely they were to postpone their first experiences with sex.

Of course, as with boys, girls who enjoy participating in sports and physical activities are more likely to keep participating. And the payoff is worth it—not just in terms of health but also in terms of confidence and even success in school. Studies show that many high school female athletes received higher grades and standardized test scores than their nonathletic counterparts. They also dropped out at lower rates and were more likely to go on to college. And female executives in *Fortune* 500 companies? Many of them were highly involved in athletics.

There's simply no good reason for parents or anyone else to discourage young girls from being physically active—and plenty of good reasons *not* to. One way in which girls and boys are the same? According to the President's Council report, numerous researchers have contended that girls aren't less athletically skilled than boys. Their activities may be different (for instance, jumping rope and performing intricate dance routines), but these activities "still require agility, coordination, strength, and attentional focus. In fact, girls possess the physical capabilities to perform well in all kinds of movement activities. What they may lack is the social support to do so."

Physical activity? Movement? Exercise? Eric Jensen simply refers to it all as *movement arts*. And writing in *Arts with the Brain in Mind*, he states:

> Movement has strong positive cognitive, emotional, social, collaborative, and neurological effects. . . . It makes strong sense that a variety of movement activities should support and sustain every child's education. In fact, it is our ethical, scientific, and health imperative that all children get mandated exposure to the movement arts.

Part II

WHAT YOU NEED TO DO

4

Starting Off on the Right Foot: Movement Experiences in Infancy

"If you were born without wings, do nothing to prevent their growing."
—Coco Chanel

IMAGINE YOU'VE JUST brought home a new kitten or puppy, which you proceed to carry around in a backpack for most of your waking hours. Then, before you go to bed, you confine it to a tiny pen. The animal gets plenty of food and water and seems perfectly content. But it has no opportunity to run and jump and frolic—as kittens and puppies typically do.

That's ridiculous, you think. *Who would do such a thing?* After all, everyone knows animals are meant to move—to play. Not only is it simply what they *do*, but also they'd grow fat and lazy—and their muscles would atrophy—if they didn't move!

Well, human animals are meant to move and play, too. The inclination—the need—is hardwired into them. Babies, in fact, spend nearly 40 percent of their waking time doing things like kicking, bouncing, and waving their arms. And while it may appear all this activity is just for the sake of moving, it's important to realize a baby is never "just moving" or "just playing." As with kittens and puppies, every action impacts the child's development in some way.

Still, recent evidence indicates that infants are spending upward of *sixty waking hours a week* constrained in things like high chairs, carriers, and car seats. How is that different from confining a kitten or puppy? Why is that less ridiculous?

The reasons for this trend are varied. For one thing, more and more infants are being placed in child-care centers, where there may not be enough space to let babies roam the floor. Or, given the number of infants enrolled, there may be little opportunity for caregivers to spend one-on-one time with each baby. So, in the morning, an infant is typically fed, dressed, and carried to the automobile, where she's placed in a car seat. She's then carried into the child-care center, where she may spend much of her time in a crib or playpen. At the end of the day, when she's picked up, she's again placed in the car seat and carried back into the house, where she's fed, bathed, and put to bed.

Even when parents and baby are home, they seem to be busier than ever these days. Who has time to get on the floor and creep around with a child? Besides, with today's emphasis on being *productive*, playing with a baby would seem almost a guilty pleasure! And if the baby seems happy and safe in a seat placed conveniently in front of the television set, in a bouncer hung in a doorway, or cruising about in a walker, what's the harm? It's a win/win situation, isn't it?

In fact, it isn't—not for the baby. Being confined or, as one colleague puts it, "containerized," affects a baby's personality; he needs to be *held*. Being confined may also have serious consequences for the child's motor and even cognitive development.

Two other trends in today's society reducing the infant's opportunities to move are the inclination to restrict, rather than encourage, freedom of movement and the misguided belief that early academic instruction will result in superbabies.

Regarding the former, consider these comments, heard frequently among and by the parents of infants: "He's so quiet; I hardly ever hear a peep from him." "She's such an easy baby—no trouble at all." "What a good boy, watching TV so nice and quiet." "You're so lucky to have such an easy-going baby."

Of course no one wants an infant who requires one's undivided attention twenty-four hours a day. Still, perhaps because we place so much importance on *busyness* in our society, we're also placing too much value on the inactivity of babies, which conveniently allows us to stay busy with other things. Thus babies are rewarded for being quiet and inactive, which is not their natural state, rather than for being energetic and lively, which is. (This is the same inclination that keeps millions of older children—many of whom are simply being kids—medicated so they'll be more passive at school.)

And then there's the whole issue of "earlier is better" when it comes to preparing children to succeed in school. Never mind that babies learn through the exploration and manipulation of their environments and the fact that they're not cognitively ready to learn in the way older children do. Many of today's parents are convinced that if they're not flashing words—in at least two different languages—in front of their baby's face, he won't get into a good preschool, which means he'll never get into the best college. And, as if the use of flash cards didn't promote enough sedentary behavior, along came the concept of computer software for babies! According to PC Data, 770,000 copies of "lapware" for infants were sold in 1999.

In this chapter we'll look at the benefits, both immediate and long-term, of letting your infant *move* and why active, rather than passive, behavior is more likely to contribute to your child's later success. We'll explore the *kind* of movement that's appropriate for babies. (What do you need to know about baby bouncers and walkers? Should you enroll your child in an infant swim or exercise program?) And you'll find lots of suggestions for what you can do at home with your infant without special training or a lot of fancy equipment.

Why Babies Need to Move

Besides the fact that they were built to do so, there are a great many reasons why infants need to move. The truth is, though their movement capabilities are extremely limited, even when compared with those of a toddler, movement experiences may be more important for infants than for children of any other age group. And it's not all about motor development either.

Thanks to new advances in brain research, we now know that early movement experiences are extremely helpful to optimal brain development. In fact early movement experiences are considered essential to the neural stimulation (the use-it-or-lose-it principle involved in the keeping or pruning of brain cells) needed for healthy brain development.

Not long ago, neuroscientists believed that the structure of a human brain was determined genetically at birth. They now realize that, although the main "circuits" are "prewired" for such functions as breathing and the beating of the heart, the *experiences* that fill each child's days are what actually determine the brain's ultimate design and, consequently, the nature and extent of that child's adult capabilities.

An infant's brain, it turns out, is chock-full of brain cells (neurons) at birth. (In fact a one-pound fetus already has a hundred billion of them!) Over time each of these brain cells can form as many as fifteen thousand connections (synapses) with other brain cells. And it is during the first three years of life that most of these connections are made. Synapses not used often enough are eliminated. On the other hand, those synapses that have been activated by repeated early experiences tend to become permanent. And it appears that physical activity and play during early childhood have a vital role in the sensory and physiological stimulation that results in more synapses.

Neurophysiologist Carla Hannaford, in her excellent book *Smart Moves: Why Learning Is Not All in Your Head*, states: "Physical movement, from earliest infancy and throughout our lives, plays an important role in the creation of nerve cell networks which are actually the essence of learning."

She then goes on to relate how movement, because it activates the neural wiring throughout the body, makes the entire body—not just the brain—the instrument of learning.

Gross (large) and fine (small) motor skills are learned through repetition as well—both by virtue of being practiced and because the repetition lays down patterns in the brain. Although it hasn't been determined clearly that such early movements as kicking, waving the arms, and rocking on hands and knees are "practice" for later, more advanced motor skills, it's believed they are indeed part of a process of neurological maturation needed for the control of motor skills. In other words these spontaneous actions prepare the child, both physically and neurologically, to later perform more complex, voluntary actions.

Then, once the child is performing voluntary actions (for example, rolling over, creeping, and walking), the circle completes itself, as these skills provide both glucose (the brain's primary source of energy) and blood flow ("food") to the brain, in all likelihood increasing neuronal connections.

According to Rebecca Anne Bailey and Elsie Carter Burton, authors of *The Dynamic Self: Activities to Enhance Infant Development*, whenever babies move any part of their bodies, there exists the potential for two different kinds of learning to occur: learning to move and moving to learn.

Why Bouncers and Walkers Don't Count

Well, you may be thinking, *all that makes sense*. You can see that Mother Nature provided us with the means and the motive to move—and that acting contrary to what nature intended may truly be a bit silly. So you determine your infant will spend as little time as possible in high chairs, carriers, and car seats.

But what about baby bouncers and baby walkers? After all, they're intended specifically for movement. They provide an infant with a lot of exercise.

Yes, in fact, they do. But, again, we have to ask whether or not it's the kind of exercise that nature intended. Your infant may seem giddy with delight as he bounces up and down, up and down, all by himself. But the truth is that these seats don't provide the kind of support required for the development of proper posture and alignment. Children with conditions like muscular dystrophy are particularly susceptible to these kinds of problems. But for all babies, too much sitting, in and of itself, may result in the deterioration of body posture.

Furthermore, infants four to eleven months aren't actually developed enough to bear weight on their lower limbs, pelvis, or lower spine. The chiropractic community is greatly concerned that such weight-bearing positions may lead to repetitive stress on these developing joints that will eventually cause orthopedic and spinal problems.

And walkers have even more going against them, in addition to lack of support for proper posture and alignment. In the early to mid-nineties, estimated annual sales of walkers were over three million—with between 55 and 92 percent of infants five to fifteen months using them. So there's no question about their popularity. But in 1993 twenty-five thousand babies were treated in hospital emergency rooms for injuries associated with the use of infant walkers. Overwhelmingly, the injuries were caused by falls, either from the walker or while the baby was still in it. From 1989 to 1993 there were eleven deaths.

As a result, in 1995, the American Academy of Pediatrics issued a policy statement explicitly recommending a ban on the manufacture and use of infant walkers in the United States. They additionally recommended that agencies responsible for licensing child-care facilities not permit the use of walkers in approved centers.

Obviously, safety is the primary motivation for this policy. But the AAP also states there are no data supporting the benefits of using walkers. On the contrary, they may impede creeping (see the next section on the importance of this motor skill) and actually delay walking by a few weeks. One study determined that frequent users of baby walkers show a *significant* delay in walking. Another found that babies who'd used walkers showed a delay not just in walking but also in sitting and creeping, and had lower scores on mental and motor development tests. And, according to the AAP, children with cerebral palsy who use walkers may "experience exaggerated abnormal motor reactions and delay in development of normal balance and protective responses."

So, although babies are more than happy to tool around in a walker or bounce endlessly while suspended in a doorway, we have to remember that babies have no idea what is and isn't good for them. We're the adults, and we must make our decisions based not on convenience or on what "everybody else is doing" but on our babies' best interests.

Getting "Down and Dirty" with Baby

It's absolutely true that stimulation is critical to a baby's development—her motor development, her brain development, all the good stuff. But that doesn't mean we have to drive ourselves crazy providing it—by programming stimulation into our already busy days or spending a lot of money on equipment and props. As Alvin Rosenfeld and Nicole Wise, in their book *Hyper-Parenting*, point out, stimulation "is built into normal, loving caregiving."

In fact, a recent report from the National Academy of Sciences called "The Science of Early Childhood Development" states:

> Given the drive of young children to master their world . . . the full range of early childhood competencies can be achieved in typical everyday environments. A cabinet of pots and pans . . . seems to serve the same purpose as a fancy, "made-for-baby" musical instrument.

Consider the natural and valuable stimulation offered by simply providing your developing infant with tummy time on the floor. Tummy time will at first encourage experimentation with lifting the head, with rolling from tummy to back and the reverse, and later, with crawling and creeping—all of which are apparently not taking place with the frequency with which they used to.

More and more pediatricians, it seems, are hearing from parents whose babies aren't lifting their heads, turning over, or creeping when the books say they should. (What's commonly known as crawling is technically creeping. Crawling is when the baby transports herself with the belly still on the floor.) The reason, they believe, is the public health campaign begun in 1994 encouraging parents to put babies to sleep on their backs to prevent sudden infant death syndrome (SIDS). Not only is this resulting in a decrease in the incidence of SIDS (certainly good news), but also infants are getting much less tummy time than did babies of previous decades (not such good news). It appears lying faceup gives babies no incentive to roll over (unlike the incentive curiosity provides when lying facedown). They often also go directly from sitting to toddling.

Pediatricians are assuring parents there's nothing to worry about—that there appear to be no medical or developmental consequences of this change in the reaching of physical milestones. The babies are normal in every other way, sitting up and walking at the same time they always did. But are these pediatricians tracking development *beyond* infancy? Do they know for certain there are no long-term effects of walking without creeping?

Carla Hannaford contends that cross-lateral movements (actions involving the left arm and right leg or the right arm and left leg at the same time, like a baby's crawling or creeping) activate both hemispheres of the brain in a balanced way. Also involved are coordinated movements of both

eyes, ears, hands, feet, and balanced core muscles. The result of all this balanced and coordinated movement is that the corpus callosum, the area
between the two hemispheres of the brain, as well as the brain's four lobes,
become more activated. According to Hannaford, this cross-hemisphere
communication heightens cognitive function and increases ease of learning.

In *Smart Moves*, Hannaford tells the story of Todd, who at sixteen years
old was unable to read—but not for lack of trying. His parents had spent
thousands of dollars on reading programs, but all had failed; Todd was certified learning disabled. Also, although he was six feet, two inches tall and
the basketball team was eager to have him participate, he was too clumsy,
unable to get from point A to point B while dribbling a ball (a bit of a prerequisite for playing hoops).

Then his mother made a discovery while at a conference in California.
That discovery was Dr. Paul Dennison's "Brain Gym" program. Very
excited, she returned home and announced, "Todd, we're going to Cross
Crawl."

Now, Cross Crawling is simply a matter of standing and slowly touching opposite elbow to knee, alternating from one side to the other. To be
sure Todd would actually do it, the whole family Cross Crawled together
every morning before Todd went to school and every night before he went
to bed. *Six weeks later*, Todd was reading at grade level. He later became a
fully participating member of the basketball team—and even later received
a college degree in biology!

Coincidence? Highly unlikely. But isn't it true, as some reading specialists insist, that the only way to learn to read is by reading? Apparently
not. Hannaford goes on to relate comparable success stories in her own
work, using these and other, similar techniques. Also, there's a great deal of
anecdotal evidence that these techniques do indeed produce results.

Why should such a simple action create such an overwhelming change?
Well, the right side of the brain controls the left side of the body, and the
left side of the brain controls the right side of the body. So, by crossing over
the midline of the body (the imaginary line running down the center of the
body, from head to toe), as is the case when touching opposite elbow to
knee, an individual prompts the two hemispheres of the brain to communicate with each other. In Todd's case, specifically, he was finally able to integrate all the knowledge that had been "up there" all along!

Physical education specialist Dr. Marjorie Corso has conducted research relevant to the brain-body connection, looking in particular at how body/space awareness transfers to paper/space awareness. For example, Corso found when she asked three- to eight-year-old children to touch their shoulders, some continually touched only one shoulder. Likewise, when asked to jump and touch the ceiling, some children reached repeatedly with only one hand.

When requesting samples of the children's papers, Corso discovered the quadrant of paper space not used in writing and coloring was the same quadrant of body space not used. She also found that children who couldn't cross the body's vertical midline tended to focus on the vertical of the paper, sometimes writing or drawing down the vertical center of the page and sometimes changing the pencil to the other hand at the midpoint of the paper. They also tended to stop reading at the middle of the page.

Why would a child be unable to cross the midline of the body—to perform an action as simple as reaching the right arm to the left side or cross-ing one ankle over the other? Many experts believe it's due to a lack of cross-lateral experience early in life—that is, crawling and creeping. And the inability to cross the midline is being seen more often these days. A teacher in a "developmental" kindergarten in upstate New York related that, at the beginning of the year, not one child in her class is able, in a single motion, to connect three Xs drawn on the chalkboard in the shape of an arc. Instead, each child connects the first two Xs with one hand and then transfers the chalk to the other hand to complete the figure.

Does this mean every child who walks before crawling will end up with learning problems? Certainly not. Just as every girl exposed to images of size-zero fashion models will not develop an eating disorder. Every child—every brain—is different. Still, there's enough evidence to indicate strongly that cross-lateral experiences are extremely important to healthy motor and cognitive development.

But don't worry if your child is no longer an infant and you believe he didn't get enough cross-lateral movement. As Todd's story shows, it's never too late to get started.

And if your child is still an infant and seems in no hurry to take that first step every parent anxiously awaits, you *really* shouldn't worry—and you shouldn't be hurrying her along! Far too many parents these days are heard boasting of the fact that their child went straight from sitting to walking. But if they were aware of how important crawling and creeping are to both motor and cognitive development, they'd realize this might be more cause for concern than for pride.

There is so much pressure in our competitive society—even for infants!—that parents are constantly monitoring the milestones of their own and others' babies. But "hurrying" milestones is a bad idea from two perspectives. First, there's no indication that reaching developmental milestones in advance of the predicted timetable means the child will *remain* advanced. (By the time your child and his peers are five, you won't be able to tell who reached the milestones first.) And hurrying a child toward a milestone may do more harm than good.

In two studies of identical twins one of each pair was taught a motor skill, like climbing stairs, and the other wasn't. In both studies the twin who *wasn't* trained learned the skill more easily when attempting it at an older age (when developmentally ready). Moreover, once the second twin had learned the skill, there was no difference in how the siblings each performed the skill.

David Elkind, in his book *Miseducation: Preschoolers at Risk*, contributes an addendum to the story of one set of twins. He reports meeting a distinguished psychiatrist who had seen this pair of twins many years after the study and declared that the twin who'd been trained early was quite different from the untrained twin. Says Elkind, "The trained twin was overly dependent on adults for direction and guidance, whereas the untrained twin demonstrated considerable autonomy."

Does this mean it's also a bad idea to provide stimulation that encourages your baby's own efforts? Definitely not. Remember, stimulating environments and experiences are vital to healthy development. But there is a difference between hurrying (prodding or training) and encouraging (offering opportunities). The former is unnatural and has more to do with the parents than the child. The latter is more *playful* in nature. It engages the child's natural instincts, and the bond between parent and child is strengthened by the interaction.

So get "down and dirty" with your baby! Place her on her tummy, with a favorite stuffed toy just out of reach, and encourage her to go get it. Make an obstacle course out of furniture tall enough to crawl under or empty

Some Motor Milestones

For the development of every motor skill there is a range of ages considered "normal." The following information should serve as a guideline only.

Birth to Six Months

- Turns head from side to side
- Follows objects and sounds with eyes
- Sits with arms propped in front for support
- Reaches for objects with both arms
- Rolls from back onto side

Six to Twelve Months

- Holds hands together
- Rolls over from front to back and reverse
- Crawls and later creeps
- Plays games like peekaboo
- Pulls self up to standing position
- Climbs stairs on hands and knees
- Walks with adult support
- Reaches for objects with one hand or the other

Twelve to Eighteen Months

- Walks without support
- Pushes, pulls, and carries objects while walking
- Able to roll and kick a large ball

---

boxes large enough to creep through. Creep right along beside her, sometimes slowly and sometimes quickly, and see how much she enjoys this simple game!

And every time other parents boast about their little darling's walking skills, just smile—because you know it makes no difference in the long run and you know there's a whole lot of synaptic activity going on in *your* little darling's brain as he happily creeps about the house!

What About Infant
Swim and Exercise Programs?

Well, then, if all this movement and stimulation is such a good idea, it only makes sense that *more* movement and stimulation—perhaps facilitated by a trained professional—is an even better idea! Not exactly.

There's no doubt infant swim programs are highly popular (about five to ten million infants and preschoolers participate in formal instruction), and infant exercise programs are becoming more so all the time. But the American Academy of Pediatrics has issued warnings about both of them. Why? We'll take a look at swim programs first.

Drowning is the leading cause of unintentional injury and death in young children, with rates highest among American children ages one to two. Still, the AAP feels strongly enough about the issue of infant swim programs that it has released two policy statements on the subject, the first in 1985 and an update in 2000.

According to the association, children are not developmentally ready for swimming lessons until they're four years old. Although they may be able to perform elementary swimming motions at about twelve months, these motions are more along the lines of a dog paddle than a traditional swimming stroke, or front crawl. And, as with other skills learned before children are developmentally ready, aquatic skills take longer to learn and are limited by the children's neuromuscular capacity. Furthermore, starting early doesn't translate into "a higher level of swimming proficiency compared with those taking lessons at a later age."

In other words, the situation is the same as it is with hurrying other motor skills. Earlier isn't better, and it's certainly not going to help create a future Olympic swimmer. Also, the training itself may have a long-term effect on the child's sense of autonomy (self-sufficiency), as motivation is an essential ingredient in the learning of any skill—and *motivation* is not yet in the infant's emotional repertoire.

But there's much more to consider here. Even when the program's intention is to focus on water safety knowledge rather than actual swimming skills (as is the intention of the aquatic programs of the YMCA and the Red Cross), caution is the key. Warns the AAP, "When instruction attempts to optimize learning by reducing fear of water, children may unwittingly be encouraged to enter the water without supervision."

Says David Elkind, in *Miseducation*, if parents enroll their babies in swim programs specifically to prevent drowning, they may unintentionally be shifting the responsibility for not drowning to the children themselves!

Furthermore, a child without the necessary cognitive skills may be unable to transfer his knowledge from one context to another. A story told recently by Kelly Ripa, cohost of "Live with Regis and Kelly," illustrates this point. Ripa was telling Regis and their audience about her family's trip to Hawaii during which her preschool son was standing in a koi pond feeding the fish. He suddenly slipped and fell facedown into the pond. But, since he'd been enrolled in swimming programs—several days a week for years— and possessed many certificates proclaiming he could swim, she and her husband merely waited for their son's swimming skills to kick in. But they never did! He remained facedown and then began to sink. It appears the child knew what was expected of him in one situation (swimming lessons) but not in an entirely new situation.

As Dr. Elkind points out, there may be other hazards as well. Infants in swimming classes are at risk for "middle-ear infections and potential permanent hearing loss, for autoasphyxiation from swallowing water, and for diarrhea, since the babies are not toilet-trained and the water may be polluted."

Similar dangers exist with infant exercise programs. Specifically, the AAP warns against programs in which the baby's limbs are exercised, held in various positions, or otherwise manipulated. While no parent would intentionally take things beyond the baby's limits, it is nonetheless all too easy to do, as an infant's bones are not completely solidified. Nor do infants have the strength or reflexes required to protect themselves from external forces—no matter how well intentioned.

And if we can try for a moment to put ourselves in the baby's "shoes," we have to wonder how all that involuntary manipulation feels. It seems it would be much like having physical therapy—certainly a necessary procedure when there's a physical problem to be addressed—but not one an individual would sign up for voluntarily!

If the purpose of the program is to provide social contact for parent and baby, that's great. If the purpose is to ensure parent and child have quality one-on-one time, during which the baby has a chance to reach for objects, creep on the floor, and rock to the rhythm of a song in Mom's or Dad's arms, that's wonderful.

But if the purpose of the program is to improve physical prowess or advance the acquisition of motor skills—well, that's territory we've already covered.

What's a Parent to Do?

State Kay Albrecht and Linda G. Miller, authors of *Innovations: Infant & Toddler Development*: "Babies who do not have experiences on the floor, moving their bodies, reaching and batting at objects, picking up many different objects, etc., may not receive enough stimulating experiences to increase synaptic coordination and communication."

Yes, many of today's babies are spending their days in child-care centers. Yes, parents are busier than ever. But this is not to imply infants are automatically at risk. As you can see from the preceding statement, providing babies with what they need is easy.

Of course, if you're considering child care, you should do whatever you can to ensure a high adult-to-child ratio. You should also be sure your caregivers are committed to giving infants plenty of opportunity to move and explore and that there are many and varied sensory experiences to be had (objects of different colors, sizes, and shapes to see and feel; sounds created by the baby himself and others to hear).

And, naturally, whether or not your baby is in or is going to be in child care, you yourself also need to sneak in as many movement experiences with her as you can!

Not surprisingly, the assumption is that, until the infant is at least able to creep, movement experiences for him are severely limited. But that's just not so. There are many ways babies can move without the ability to transport themselves from place to place (for example, kicking, reaching, rolling over). There are also a number of physical experiences babies should have in preparation for later movement activities (for instance, activities promoting visual tracking and eye-hand coordination). Following are several suggestions. Keep in mind that these are suggestions only. You should feel free to adapt them to your own baby's needs.

For example, as you choose activities to do with your baby, consider providing a variety of opportunities based on her level of skill development. You'll want to offer activities she can easily master, as well as those that provide practice in areas still developing. Remember, too, that repetition is essential in early childhood. Repeat your baby's favorite activities as often as possible. You'll tire of them well before she will!

While you're playing, use language with the baby—describing what you're doing and what he's doing or seeing and delighting in his accomplishments. Not only will this provide motivation; it will also promote your baby's language development.

Also, some babies prefer a quiet approach to activity while others prefer a higher level of stimulation, which will affect the nature of your playtime. Your baby may even alternate between the two, responding one time to a subdued style and another time to a more vigorous one. If you're sensitive to your infant's moods and energy levels, plan to play only when she's well-rested and happy and sense when she's had enough. There's a greater chance you'll help instill a *love* of physical activity at this early age.

Finally, Dr. Marilyn Segal, author of *Your Child at Play: Birth to One Year*, recommends making play with the baby a family affair. She writes, "You will discover very soon that every member of your family has his or her own style of playing. It is good for your baby to experience these differences." She further reminds parents that "the most important outcome of every activity is the reinforcement of a warm and loving relationship."

Now, here are some activities.

- **Rolling Over.** Babies' first movements are reflexive, or involuntary. Rolling over is a voluntary movement—and one you can encourage by providing a little incentive. While the baby is lying on his back, sit behind him, holding a small toy over his head. Once you have the baby's attention, move the toy very slowly to one side, all the while encouraging him to get it. If the baby rolls over, present him with the toy. You can then repeat the game on the other side.

- **Visual Tracking.** Provide your baby with bright, colorful objects to watch. Finger puppets or a brightly colored sock placed on your hand can be used to gain and keep the baby's attention. Then slowly move your hand up and down, in circles, and to the right and left. Blow bubbles for the baby to watch (making sure they're far enough away so they don't pop in her face). When the baby's old enough, encourage her to reach for the bubbles—or any other object of desire you place above her. Play "sound" games with your baby, too. Shake a rattle or other noise-producing object above the baby's head or to her side, encouraging her to locate the sound. This provides practice with both visual tracking and sound discrimination.

- **Body Awareness.** As with older children, body awareness is essential for babies. Sing and demonstrate "Where Is Thumbkin?" Play games like "This Little Piggy" with both toes and fingers. Touch her nose, exclaiming, "I've got your nose!" Then proceed to play the game with such other body parts as toes, ears, fingers, and legs. When the baby's developmentally ready, ask her to find *your* nose, ears, mouth, and so on.

   Games like patty-cake have lasted through the years because they work so well with infants. They offer opportunities for social interaction, imitation, touch, and rhythmic awareness—and yet another chance for baby to hear your voice.

- **Individuation.** There's nothing like the tried-and-true game of peekaboo to help the child begin to see himself as a separate individual. It also makes babies laugh! Once the baby is familiar with this game, you can move on to "Where's Mommy [Daddy, Nana, etc.]?" Begin by placing your hands over your face, just as you would with peekaboo. Later, hide your whole self behind a piece of furniture, asking, "Where's Mommy?" You then pop up, answering, "*Here's* Mommy!"

- **Crossing the Midline.** To encourage crossing the midline of the body, hand your baby desirable items in such a way that she has to reach *across* her body to retrieve them from you. Later, when the baby is crawling and creeping, place a brightly colored object or favorite toy on the floor, just out of reach, encouraging her to go get it. Then, as long as she seems to enjoy the game (she's laughing instead of fussing), keep moving it.

- **Eye-Hand Coordination.** Any activity in which the baby is reaching for or batting an object promotes eye-hand coordination. Another option, appropriate for infants as young as three months, is to sew a bell or bells onto an elastic band that you can slip on your baby's wrists or ankles. Once on, gently shake the body part until the baby looks at it.

  Also, when your baby is able to sit unassisted, make him comfortable on the floor, legs apart. Sit opposite him in a similar manner and roll a large, brightly colored ball toward him. Describe what you're doing and encourage him to push it back toward you.

  Put warm water in a large, unbreakable bowl placed on the floor and encourage the baby to touch and splash the water. Another possibility is giving her two large paper or plastic cups, one of which is filled with dry cereal, and encouraging her to pour the cereal from one cup to the other. Since both of these tend to be messy activities, it's best to first prepare the floor area with a large vinyl tablecloth.

- **Manipulative Skills.** Motor skills in which an object is typically manipulated (usually by the hands or the feet) are known as *manipulative skills*. Throwing, catching, and kicking fall into this category.

  To provide opportunities for kicking, place a stuffed animal or a small pillow by your baby's feet, close enough to touch, and encourage her to kick away. Give her plenty of soft objects to throw as well, retrieving them for her as long as she stays interested. Once she's walking, you can place an empty laundry basket on the floor and suggest she toss soft balls, rolled-up socks, or similar items into the basket.

  Although your baby won't have the visual tracking or eye-hand coordination skills to successfully catch objects for quite a while, you can promote the development of these skills by tossing bright, colorful scarves into the air and encouraging him to catch them. (Chiffon scarves work best since they tend to float the most slowly.) You'll have to begin by demonstrating yourself, but eventually the baby will want to try to catch them, too.

- **Imitation.** Babies are great at mimicking, and at about ten months of age they have a greater understanding of what they're doing and really enjoy it. Surprisingly enough, imitating is an important skill, as the ability to physically replicate what the eyes are seeing comes in handy later for things like writing and drawing. Also, imitation helps confirm for babies that they're like other people.

  Play the mirror game with your baby while sitting and facing each other. Stick out your tongue, wiggle your fingers in your ears, wave your arms up and down, all while encouraging the baby to do likewise. When your baby is ready to figure out how the game is played, encourage *him* to lead while you imitate.

  Later, when your baby is mobile, "Follow the Leader" is a wonderful game to play. It will encourage imitating while also providing practice with walking. Be sure to vary the speed of your movements, the pathways you take (possibilities are straight, curving, and zigzagging), and your body's shape (big, small, wide, etc.).

- **Cruising.** As mentioned, hurrying skills like standing or walking is never a good idea. Babies will get to these skills when they're developmentally ready, but they do need to be given opportunities. Toward this end you can be sure your baby has chances to pull herself up on *sturdy* furniture, like a sofa or heavy coffee table. If you notice she's trying to pull herself up with something that's not sturdy, you can simply pick her up and put her someplace more appropriate. (Be aware, however, that once she's up, she may need your help getting back down!) Eventually she'll begin to "walk," using the furniture for support.

  Once he's walking unassisted, your baby will enjoy pushing, pulling, and carrying objects while walking. Not only does this provide practice with this locomotor skill, but also it helps develop understanding of cause and effect.

In *Active Start: A Statement of Physical Activity Guidelines for Children Birth to Five Years* (see Appendix A), the National Association for Sport and Physical Education has issued five guidelines relevant to infants. The first three are:

1. Infants should interact with parents and/or caregivers in daily physical activities that are dedicated to promoting the exploration of their environment.

2. Infants should be placed in safe settings that facilitate physical activity and do not restrict movement for prolonged periods of time.

3. Infants' physical activity should promote the development of movement skills.

By playing the simple games described here, and others like them, you can easily meet the objectives of these guidelines *and* deepen the bond between you and your infant.

5

Promoting Your Child's
Motor Development

"Many things can wait. Children cannot. . . . To them we cannot say tomorrow. Their name is today."
—GABRIELLA MISTRAL, NOBEL PRIZE–WINNING POET

A STUDY INVOLVING parents and teachers in fifteen countries found the majority of them believe the development of motor skills is important for their children. However, they evidently also assume motor skill development happens without adult intervention—because neither the parents nor the teachers felt it was their responsibility to promote it. Nor did they feel it was the responsibility of the other group.

Most people, it seems, believe children automatically acquire motor skills as their bodies develop—that it's a natural, "magical" process that occurs along with maturation. Unfortunately, this is an easy assumption to make. After all, one day the infant rolls over by herself, eventually starts to crawl, and then suddenly rises up onto hands and knees and begins creeping. Somewhere around her first birthday, with only a little assistance and a lot of enthusiastic encouragement from you, she takes her first steps. And then it seems, almost before you know it, she's off and running!

So it certainly *appears* that motor skills miraculously occur and pretty much take care of themselves. And, to a certain extent, it's true. However, maturation takes care of only part of the process—the part that allows a child to execute most movement skills at an immature level.

What does an *immature level* mean? Consider the phrase "She throws like a girl" and the even more insulting phrase "*He* throws like a girl." Regardless of which gender the words are directed at, they refer to a child who hasn't achieved a mature performance level for the skill of throwing. Something about the child's form or technique isn't quite right. And, believe it or not, it can happen with such basic motor skills as running. (Have you ever observed a child who hadn't quite mastered the ability to move limbs in perfect opposition? Or whose feet roll in, baby toes lifting off the ground?)

The truth is, thanks to the mistaken notion that children don't need help in this area, many children never achieve mature patterns for many motor skills. As evidence of this, an Australian study of twelve hundred students between the ages of five and twelve found an "appalling" level of ability in basic motor skills. Among the findings:

- Only about 45 percent of elementary school students can catch with correct form.
- The eleven-year-old boys were best able to perform a vertical jump, but only 11 percent of them could do it properly.
- Only 2 to 3 percent of the twelve-year-olds could hit a softball or baseball correctly.
- Fewer than 10 percent of the children were able to run correctly.

That truly is appalling. But why should we care? After all, it's not as though motor skills are as valuable in life as language skills (for which we do provide instruction).

Well, maybe not in all areas of life. But they certainly are in some.

The Importance of Movement Skills

There are two general types of motor skills: fine and gross. The former refers to "small" motor skills, or movement skills using small muscles, such as writing, drawing, and cutting paper with scissors. The latter indicates "large" motor skills, or movement skills using large muscles, like running and jumping. These are the subject of this chapter.

Consider the words of physical education specialists Gina V. Barton, Kim Fordyce, and Kym Kirby, writing in a publication for PE teachers, *Teaching Elementary Physical Education*:

> Motor skills are not only critical life skills that enable us to go about our daily lives effectively and safely; motor skills are also important determinates of our ability to participate in our culture, and develop and maintain a physically active lifestyle. Motor skills enable children to participate in the kinds of movement that contribute to their physical and cognitive growth. Competence in motor skills is important to the positive emotional development of children.

The preceding paragraph touches on the role of motor skills in the child's physical, social/emotional, and cognitive domains. So once again reference is made to movement's impact on the development of the whole—thinking, feeling, moving—child. Let's delve into it a bit further.

Obviously, the ability to perform gross motor skills is related directly to physical fitness. And, considering the health hazards for the unfit (detailed in Chapter 1), this is one area where movement matters more than language. A *competent* mover will gladly keep moving. A child—or an adult (poor movement habits do track from childhood)—who feels physically awkward and uncoordinated is simply going to avoid movement at all costs. (Just as a person who feels inept at public speaking will avoid a podium at all costs.)

Perhaps you recall a child from physical education class—or perhaps you *were* that child—who went to extremes to sit out, even going so far as to fake injury or illness. True, physical education class makes up a very small percentage of a child's life. But how likely is it that such a child would then take part in an after-school game of tag? Or play jump rope or climb the monkey bars during recess? How likely is it that his parents would even consider taking him to a playground on the weekend, when he finds movement distasteful? There's no mystery as to why the research shows children lacking in movement fundamentals are three times more sedentary than peers of the same age who are skilled movers.

Additionally, children (even preschoolers) tend to be movement "snobs"—a fact that impacts both their social and emotional development.

Studies show that physical skill is positively associated with peer acceptance and leadership among adolescents and elementary-school students. Even the five- and six-year-olds with the highest levels of motor skills were more popular than those with the lowest levels, especially among the boys. It makes sense, really: the more skilled children are, the more they engage in physical play, which grants them greater opportunities for social interaction. And along with it all come confidence and higher levels of self-esteem.

That addresses the physical and social/emotional domains. What about the cognitive? Well, research shows that children confident in their physical coordination develop greater proficiency in writing and reading. And, of course, Chapter 3 detailed numerous other ways in which physical activity further impacts the cognitive domain.

So, yes, motor skills are critical to a child's overall development—and to many significant aspects of life. What parent wouldn't want her child to move well so as to be physically fit, self-confident, intelligent, and popular? What parent wouldn't want his child to grow up with the advantages that mastery of motor skills offers? But how best to make this happen?

Fundamentals First

Would you hand your child calculus problems once she was able to count to ten? A geometry text when he began to recognize shapes? *War and Peace* as soon as she could recite her ABCs? Of course not! Not only is it preposterous to have such expectations of a child, but also it sets the child up for failure—and, most likely, a dread of and distaste for calculus, geometry, and reading.

Yet all too many parents don't think twice about enrolling their young children in gymnastics, karate, dance classes, and organized sports before their kids have mastered such basic movements as bending and stretching, walking with correct posture, and bouncing and catching a ball. How is that significantly different from expecting a child who's barely learned to speak to clearly recite the Declaration of Independence—for an audience, no less?

The fact that your little one can walk doesn't necessarily mean he's ready to successfully—or fearlessly—walk a balance beam. Because your toddler is flexible enough to get her big toe into her mouth, that doesn't mean she's ready for ballet's pliés and relevés. Even if your five-year-old can run circles around you, it doesn't mean he's prepared to simultaneously run and dribble a ball in a game of soccer. And how much sense does it make to enroll your eight-year-old in competitive softball while she's still demonstrating an improper throwing form?

The basic motor skills—nonlocomotor (stationary, like bending and stretching), locomotor (traveling, like walking or hopping), and manipulative (object control, like bouncing and catching a ball)—have been called the *ABCs of movement*. And, just as we wouldn't expect children to begin reading without the ability to identify the letters of the alphabet, we shouldn't expect children to take part in certain structured physical activities without first experiencing success with the ABCs of movement.

Movements—from the simple to the complex—are like building blocks. You must have the foundation laid before you can construct the ground floor. You've got to have the ground floor completed before the rest of the building can be erected. Similarly, a logical progression of motor skills is essential if children are to achieve optimal motor development. If they skip the prerequisites, they may never progress successfully from one level of skill development to the next.

Moreover, bad habits acquired early in life are likely to persist throughout an entire lifetime. For example, the young pitcher who hasn't yet acquired a mature level of throwing isn't likely to lose his bad habits simply because he's required to pitch one or two games a week. Rather, the odds are these bad habits will simply become more and more ingrained as time goes on—a situation that could have ripple-effect consequences for years to come. He could, for instance, develop shoulder problems that prevent him not only from pitching in high school and beyond but also from taking part in recreational and fitness activities as an adult.

In Chapter 3 we explored the increasingly accepted theory of critical periods. In the course of a lifetime it is from the prenatal period through age five that children acquire and best learn the basic motor skills. The most sensible course of action, therefore, is to ensure children learn them *correctly* during this period. The least sensible strategy is for children to learn incorrectly or only to a certain, low level and expect them to correct their errors or improve their skill level merely because they age chronologically.

Motor Milestones

In Chapter 4 some approximate motor milestones for children birth to eighteen months were offered. Here we'll look at some of the motor milestones for children eighteen months to eight years. Remember, these are general guidelines only; you shouldn't become overly concerned if your child hasn't acquired one of these skills by the age listed.

Eighteen to Twenty-Four Months

- Walks forward, backward, and sideways
- Runs with stops and starts, but unable to stop and start quickly
- Climbs stairs
- Jumps up and down, but often falls

Twenty-Four to Thirty Months

- Ascends and descends stairs alone
- Steps in place
- Rolls a ball
- Bends easily at waist without toppling over
- Runs in a rudimentary fashion
- Jumps forward with two-foot takeoff
- Lifts in a rudimentary fashion

Thirty to Thirty-Six Months

- Walks on tiptoe
- Balances momentarily on one foot
- Jumps in place without falling
- Jumps off objects
- Kicks large stationary ball
- Pushes/pulls an object or person (twenty-four to thirty-six months)

Three to Four Years

- Changes speed, direction, or style of movement at signal
- Walks a straight line and low balance beam
- Runs on tiptoes
- Throws object without losing balance; can throw underarm

- Gallops
- Hops briefly
- Uses alternate feet to ascend stairs
- Catches a large or bounced ball with both arms extended
- Jumps to floor from approximately twelve inches
- Performs a forward roll

Four to Five Years

- Starts, stops, turns, and moves easily around obstacles and others (well oriented in space)
- Hops on nondominant foot
- Crosses feet over midline of body
- Descends stairs with alternate feet
- Jumps over objects five to six inches high
- Leaps over objects ten inches high
- Bounces and catches a ball
- Sometimes skips on one side only
- Performs a backward roll
- Throws with basic overarm pattern
- Catches by trapping ball to chest
- Lifts with proper form: back straight, head up, legs doing the work

Five to Six Years Old

- Slides
- Skips using alternate feet
- Catches a thrown ball with hands, though not always successfully
- Balances on either foot
- Shifts body weight to throw ("steps out" with foot opposite throwing hand)
- Kicks a rolling ball
- Bounces a ball with one hand

Six to Eight Years

- Performs most gross motor skills
- Executes two skills concurrently (for example, running and catching)

Writing in the *International Journal of Physical Education*, motor development specialist and professor Carl Gabbard states: "In contemporary motor development literature, the period of early childhood is associated with the fundamental movement phase of motor behavior. This is a unique period in the lifespan due primarily to the emergence of fundamental movement abilities which establish the foundation upon which more complex movement skills are possible later in life."

In other words, fundamentals first. Children should walk before they run. They should bend and stretch before they twist and dodge. They should throw for distance before throwing for accuracy. Static movement (balancing on tiptoes or hitting a ball off a tee) should precede dynamic movement (walking a balance beam or hitting a pitched ball). And children should definitely succeed at single actions (like bouncing a ball) before attempting combinations of them (simultaneously running and bouncing a ball).

Still, a study conducted at Northern Kentucky University found that almost half (49 percent) of children ages five to eight lacked the *minimum* skills necessary to play organized sports. And yet there are millions of five- to eight-year-old—not to mention three- and four-year-old—children who are playing (or trying to play) organized sports. There are millions of others participating in dance, gymnastics, karate, and more who similarly lack the requisite skills.

Of course, if your child is involved in sports, dance, gymnastics, and such—and you'd like her to stay involved—you have even more reason to ensure she's able to successfully perform the fundamentals. First, they're the prerequisites to sport-specific, dance, and gymnastic skills. If a child can't perform a skill required by her chosen activity, the chances are excellent she hasn't sufficiently learned a prerequisite skill.

Second—and perhaps more important—children who are successful in physical activities *continue* in those physical activities and others as well. Children who can't yet catch successfully but are nonetheless put into an outfield will soon learn to panic at the sight of an approaching ball. Children without the necessary eye-foot coordination (most children under the age of nine or ten), who are nonetheless expected to make and maintain contact with a soccer ball, will more often feel frustration than pride. Children who can't yet walk with grace and balance, who are nonetheless placed onstage and required to perform ballerina-like, will feel embarrassment at their shortcomings, even if they're not yet consciously aware of what they are. And then what happens? Physical activity comes to be associated with shame and discomfort, not joy and exhilaration.

How does a child move from an immature level of skill development to a higher level? The same way one gets to Carnegie Hall: practice, practice, practice! According to the American Academy of Pediatrics: "During the preschool years, motor skills are best learned in an unstructured, non-competitive setting in which a child can experiment and learn by trial and error on an individual basis. Specific skills can be refined through repetitive practice only after the relevant level of motor development has been reached." (In other words, we shall attempt no skill before its time.)

How much practice? That depends. A number of factors are involved, including prior experience, physical maturity, level of cognitive development, amount and kind of instruction, and the child's own motivation. In general, however, research has discovered it takes somewhere between 240 and 600 minutes of instruction for the average student to become proficient in one basic movement skill. In one study the children involved began to throw at a mature level after a *year and a half* of instruction and more than 400 trials.

As Joan Lawson puts it so simply in the *Journal of Physical Education, Recreation & Dance*: ". . . children need instruction, encouragement, and a lot of practice to achieve mature stages of [a] skill."

If you find this a bit overwhelming and perhaps even discouraging, please remember: a child's development is not a race. Besides, given the time and opportunity, your child will happily agree to repeated practice with only a little encouragement. That's because, once a child learns a new skill, he's so pleased with himself he's naturally inclined to perform it over and over and over again.

Great Expectations

Most parents haven't had training in motor development, so it's certainly understandable if you don't know what to expect as your children mature in this way. How are you to know if your expectations are remotely within reason? Or if you may be doing your child some harm, psychologically or even physically?

While it's true that motor development is a vast and technical subject, the fact is you don't need to be a motor development expert to do right by your child in this area. What you do need is patience, a basic understanding of motor skills, and a realistic grasp of the process involved in acquiring them. You'll eventually also want to make sure your child has developmentally appropriate physical education classes incorporating instruction in motor skills (see Chapter 7) and, should he have motor coordination problems, the help of experts in addition to the PE specialist.

But first, let's consider what you can do on your own, beginning with a general understanding of the process.

Not only does each child move through stages of development; each individual skill does, too. That is, as a child learns each new skill, she'll first perform it imperfectly. With time, instruction, and practice, she'll continue to perform this skill better and better until, hopefully, she's able to execute it competently. But, when introduced to yet another skill, she'll have to repeat the process—at first performing it rather awkwardly, gradually improving, and eventually mastering it.

Physical education specialist Glenn Kirchner uses learning to ride a bicycle to explain the process involved in acquiring a new motor skill. If you think back, you'll probably recall how unsteady your initial attempts were and how much concentration the effort required. Gradually you became more proficient at keeping the bike upright. But stopping and turning—different skills entirely—still required effort and concentration.

Similarly, when a child first learns to walk, it takes tremendous effort and concentration just to remain erect. With practice gravity is overcome, but the baby still requires a wide stance to feel secure. With more practice the baby's position improves until the feet are moving side by side, arms swinging in opposition, with upright posture and weight distributed evenly over all five toes, which are pointed straight ahead. The motion becomes automatic and efficient. (This, at least, is the goal. And please note: *if* completed satisfactorily, this is a process that takes a good many months.)

When the child begins to run, however, he won't automatically achieve a mature form simply because he's able to walk proficiently. Because running is a much more demanding skill, gravity will once again prove to be a challenge, as will posture and coordination.

Different physical education texts use different terms to describe the process involved in moving through these stages. Kirchner labels the stages *initial, intermediate,* and *automatic.* The first, as he describes it, involves as much thinking about a skill as trying to perform it. The intermediate phase represents a gradual shift from acquiring the fundamentals of the skill to a more focused effort to refine it. In the final phase the skill feels and looks automatic.

David Gallahue of Indiana University describes essentially the same three phases of motor learning and labels them the *initial stage,* the *elementary stage,* and the *mature stage.* And George Graham, Shirley Holt/ Hale, and Melissa Parker, in *Children Moving,* have chosen four categories to describe what they call "generic levels of skill proficiency." The first, the precontrol level, represents the stage at which a child is unable to either "consciously control or intentionally replicate a movement." They use the example of a child's initial attempts to bounce a ball, during which the child spends more time chasing it than bouncing it. The ball, rather than the child, seems to be in control. At the control (advanced beginner) level the movement is much closer to the child's actual intentions, although a good deal of concentration is still required. When children reach the utilization level in a particular skill, they don't have to think as much about how to execute the skill and are able to use it in different contexts (as in a game). The proficiency level is the advanced stage and represents the level at which a movement appears effortless and an individual is able to use it in changing environments and repeat it with ever-increasing degrees of quality.

Why do you need to know this stuff? So you can keep your expectations on the realistic side of the scale.

For each new skill learned, your child will begin at (adopting the terminology of Graham et al.) the precontrol level. Then, depending on the skill involved, it will be a good long time before she's moved through the control level and on to the utilization level—ready to actually *use* the skill in a situation as dynamic (unpredictable) as a game. And just so you know: the experts agree that elementary-aged students never reach the proficiency level for most motor skills!

But don't get the impression that motor skill development is age-dependent—a mistaken belief too many parents share because they've seen charts outlining the ages at which children should reach certain developmental milestones. Motor development is merely age-*related*. A child isn't automatically at the utilization level simply because she's eight years old. Nor would it be correct to assume that all middle-schoolers, for example, are adept at all the basic motor skills and are ready to take them to the next level—just because they're eleven or twelve.

As Nancy E. Sayre and Jere Dee Gallagher point out in *The Young Child and the Environment*, age alone is not an agent of change. Age merely marks a passage of time. It's what *happens* during that passage of time that determines a child's readiness to move on to the next level of development.

Where infants are concerned, new findings suggest that only broad guidelines for developmental milestones are useful to parents. It simply serves no purpose to employ the label *early* or *late* in relation to a baby's motor development because it doesn't matter how quickly the baby gets to each milestone—just so long as he gets there. Children usually move through the same sequence of skills, but they do so at their own pace. Even among siblings, comparison serves no purpose. If Sarah walks at nine months old and Michael at thirteen months, a few years down the road no one will be able to tell who reached this developmental milestone first. Just as development is not a race, there's no award for crossing the "finish line" ahead of everyone else.

Yes, it's natural for you to assume your child is far superior to others his age—"ahead of the game," as it were. But the fact is you can't judge your child's future athletic, tap-dancing, or acrobatic ability by how early he walks—or gallops or skips!

Conversely, you shouldn't worry if your child's development doesn't seem to be progressing as smoothly as it should. Children develop in spurts, with occasional delays a natural part of the process. Even from one day to the next, their performance can be unpredictable—as Sayre and Gallagher write, fairly skilled one day and the next day appearing as though they're practicing for the first time. If this is the case—and the situation and environment have remained unchanged—it may be due to something as simple as fatigue or boredom. Or it may be due to nothing you can detect at all.

Over the long run Kenneth Cooper also cautions parents to be aware of what he calls the "catch-up effect." For example, in *Fit Kids!*, he states many eight-, nine-, or ten-year-old children are less capable in sports than others their age. But by the time they turn twelve, thirteen, or fourteen—or, in some cases, sixteen or seventeen—"they not only catch up, but also they are sometimes in a position to surpass the same classmates who seemed hopelessly far ahead of them years before."

Dr. Cooper refers to being "in a position" to catch up with and surpass classmates because, too often, parents and coaches have given up on these kids too soon. If they've been discouraged in any way, they fail to keep working on their skills and never get the chance to catch up.

There are any number of factors that influence the pace of a child's motor development. Mentioned earlier were prior experience, physical maturity, level of cognitive development, instruction, and the child's own motivation. Also: How heavy is the child? (For example, heavy babies generally walk later than lighter babies.) How strong is the child? (A larger, stronger preschooler will throw the ball farther than a smaller, slighter preschooler.) How much practice has the child had (in a fun, natural, noncompetitive setting that doesn't eventually result in practice burnout)?

Gender, it turns out, has relatively little to do with movement abilities—physically at least. For a number of motor skills, males tend to be only slightly more advanced than females during the preadolescent years. But it's unclear how much of the difference is due to parental expectations and encouragement (as pointed out in Chapter 3). Even throwing ability, which is generally greater in males than females, can be attributed to gender expectations. One researcher contends that, among other things, girls are taught to take up less space than are boys. (Any female who's had to relinquish both armrests when seated between two males on a plane can identify with that.) As a result a girl tends to use only her throwing arm—as opposed to her entire body—to propel an object.

The bottom line in motor development is this: the National Association for Sport and Physical Education (NASPE) maintains that a physically educated person "demonstrates competence in many movement forms and proficiency in a few movement forms." And, in standards the association has devised for physical educators, it calls for younger children to demonstrate "progress toward the mature form" of the *basic* skills—and for *sixth-graders* to have achieved a mature form so they can use these skills in applied settings (like game play).

The meaning in terms of your expectations? First, children shouldn't be required to be great at *all* movement skills (just as a gifted pianist shouldn't also be expected to be a brilliant flutist). Second, for the first several years of your child's life, all you need to focus on is *progress toward the mature form*.

In short, you can't allow the "superkid syndrome" to take over. Incorrect interpretations of information in this section include: if a little bit of practice is good, then a lot must be better, and *lots more* would be better still; and if it takes a year and a half to learn to throw correctly, I should get my child started as early as humanly possible! To reiterate points made previously: your child should start when developmentally ready, and readiness includes having mastered the prerequisite skills.

Concerned that your daughter doesn't yet have the gymnastic skills of Mary Lou Retton or your son the ice-skating skills of Scott Hamilton? Don't be. What you should be looking at instead is how well he or she is walking, running, and jumping—that is, performing the fundamentals. If your child is talented in a certain area—and interested enough—the rest will come eventually.

When Should I Worry?

As a parent you often worry about your child's development—in all areas. Where motor development is concerned, your worries may be a result of comparing your child with others of the same age. You may be unaware that, for each developmental milestone, there's a range of ages considered normal.

Sometimes, however, parents' concerns are legitimate; and they're the first to identify delayed motor development, particularly during the baby's first year.

Fortunately, serious motor control problems are fairly rare. According to the pediatricians at keepkidshealthy.com, only about 3 percent of children will fail to attain milestones "on time." And, of those, only 15 to 20 percent will actually be developing abnormally.

But, according to Nancy Sornson, teacher consultant at Miller Early Childhood Center in Brighton, Michigan, and founder of Motor Moms & Dads, schools are seeing more children with motor skill delays—and who don't know the limits of their own personal space—all the time.

Sornson says there are a number of reasons for this, including the increasing number of premature babies being saved by modern medicine, many of whom are slightly injured. However, she believes the primary reason for motor delays and children bumping into each other is that children simply aren't moving as much as they used to. Their sedentary lifestyles aren't giving them the practice they need either with motor skills or personal space. Furthermore, inactivity can cause obesity and low muscle tone. Either of these conditions can then result in difficulty walking, running, skipping, and jumping. And they create children who tire easily!

Still, unlike language delays, motor skill delays can be difficult to detect. If your child is a bit awkward and uncoordinated in his movements, it could be due to slight motor delays—or he may just be clumsy. Clumsiness, like other traits, can be inherited—built into the genes. Similarly, what you assume to be a problem may just be due to lack of maturity rather than poor motor coordination. The AAP points out that preschoolers have yet to adequately acquire a number of movement skills (citing that, among four-year-olds, only 20 percent are able to throw well and only 30 percent can catch well). Accordingly, if your preschooler regularly drops the ball when you throw it to her, you shouldn't rush to the conclusion that she's experiencing delays.

You should also be aware that some delays are situational. A child may temporarily experience delays if there are problems in the household—like parental depression or discord. Once the situation is resolved, so too are the motor delays.

When should you be concerned? The pediatricians at keepkidshealthy .com say your infant *may* not be developing normally if he's not able to:

- Bring his hands together by four months
- Roll over by six months

- Support his head when pulled to a sitting position after six months
- Sit by himself without support by eight months
- Creep by twelve months
- Walk by fifteen months

For older children, you should be concerned if:

- After lots of practice in nonstressful, noncompetitive situations, your child's performance shows no sign of improvement
- Your child is *noticeably* behind other children her age
- She demonstrates an obvious stiffness or awkwardness in her movements
- She frequently trips, falls, or bumps into things
- She displays a setback in her movement abilities, such as suddenly becoming a stumbler while doing things she used to do well, like walking or climbing stairs—or becoming completely unable to do things she could do previously

If any of these conditions are present, you should certainly consult your pediatrician for an evaluation to determine whether the delays are situational, as mentioned earlier, or caused by something permanent and unchangeable. (Falling into the latter category are cerebral palsy, autism, and mental retardation, which is usually identified before the child is three, and muscular dystrophy, which can appear during the preschool years.) If the situation is permanent, your doctor (or an occupational or physical therapist) will work with the child to bring his skills to the highest level possible.

Some motor delays have no identifiable cause. But the most important thing for you to know is that, whatever the cause, motor delays do not simply go away on their own. If you suspect your child has a problem with certain skills, the first thing you can do is make sure she gets more practice. For example, if she's having trouble with alternating movements, like climbing or descending stairs, play games with repetitive movement patterns, like hopscotch. And make sure the practice is fun! If it feels like therapy or work, your child will lose any incentive she may have had.

You also want to be very careful not to label him in any way. If he hears you referring to him as "clumsy," "uncoordinated," or "a klutz"—or if you suggest he not play the games other children are playing—he might shy away from the physical activity that could help him overcome his problems.

What's a Parent to Do?

So, assuming there are no serious motor problems present, what can you, as an involved parent, do to help promote your child's motor development? To help ensure she becomes a competent, confident mover who enjoys and therefore takes part in physical activity? The answer is: plenty!

As stated earlier, practice is one of the most important factors involved in achieving higher levels of skill performance. But one of the most important factors involved in practice is that it not feel like practice!

It's simple, really: all you have to do is play with your child. It should be noncompetitive play, with no pressure whatsoever, and your child should never guess you're trying to "improve" her.

Following are some other general tips to keep in mind:

- Keep the sessions short. It's better to have shorter, more frequent sessions than to wear your child out with a few that seem never-ending.

- Build on skills in a logical order (see the sidebar listing categories of movement skills). Remember, too, that performing a skill in a stationary environment precedes performing it in a moving environment. An example is catching a ball tossed to oneself versus catching one hit by a bat.

- If you're using equipment (for instance, a bat and ball), be sure it's child-sized. Equipment meant for adults can seriously stack the odds against a child.

- Keep a progression in mind for equipment, too. For instance, if you're working on catching, start with something simple and nonthreatening that allows for maximum success, like a chiffon scarf. Then work your way up from there, perhaps with a balloon, followed by a small beach ball and then increasingly smaller (soft, easily grasped) balls.

- Children need to work on a skill as a whole before attempting its smaller parts. For example, a child needs to feel comfortable with a vertical jump as a whole before she can begin to concentrate on toe-ball-heel landings or the role her arms can play in achieving greater height.

- Be sure your child is dressed in clothing that allows for maximum movement and the possibility of dirtying.

- Whenever possible, demonstrate a skill yourself so your child has an opportunity to see what it should look like. Children need to employ as many senses in the learning process as possible.

There are two other things children need as they practice their motor skills: variety and feedback. Variety truly is the spice of life and can help ensure you and your child remain interested and challenged. It will also ensure that your child gets to experience the full range of possibilities for each movement.

To achieve this, you should keep in mind the various elements of movement. If we speak of these elements in terms of grammar, they're the movement "adverbs," while the skills themselves (creeping, shaking, climbing, etc.) are the movement "verbs." In other words the elements of movement modify—or change—*how* the movement skills are performed.

To demonstrate, let's use the locomotor skill ("verb") of walking. If this skill were being explored, there'd be quite a few choices as to how to perform it. You and your child could walk forward, backward, to the side, or in straight, curving, or zigzagging pathways (the movement element of *space* is at work here). You could perform it with arms, head, or body held in various positions (the element of *shape*), quickly or slowly (*time*), heavily or lightly (*force*), with or without interruptions (*flow*), or to the accompaniment of a song or drumbeat (*rhythm*).

Not all of the elements can be applied to every skill, of course. But, when possible, you should run through the options in your mind. Can the skill be performed in different directions, at different levels, or along varying pathways? Can you change the body's shape while performing it? (The answer: only if it means the skill can still be executed correctly.) Can

Categories of Motor Skills

These skills are listed in a general developmental progression.

Locomotor Skills

- Crawl
- Creep
- Walk
- Run
- Jump
- Leap
- Gallop
- Hop
- Slide
- Skip

Nonlocomotor Skills

- Stretch
- Bend
- Sit
- Shake
- Turn
- Rock/Sway
- Swing
- Twist
- Dodge

Manipulative Skills

- Pulling
- Pushing
- Lifting
- Throwing
- Kicking
- Ball rolling
- Volleying
- Bouncing
- Catching
- Striking
- Dribbling (with the feet)

Gymnastic Skills

- Rolling
- Transferring weight
- Balancing
- Climbing
- Hanging and swinging

it be performed at different speeds or with varying amounts of force? Does the element of flow apply? (Hop-hop-stop, hop-hop-stop is an example of bound, or interrupted, flow.) Does it make sense to try it to the accompaniment of different rhythms? (A gallop and a skip each have a distinctive rhythm, so in the case of these two locomotor skills, the answer would be no.)

Variety also applies to the environment in which a child gets to move. You should, of course, make sure your child has enough play space at home—both inside and outside—to explore plenty of movement possibilities. But you'll also want to ensure he has a chance to practice skills on different surfaces, in different kinds of spaces, and with different kinds of equipment.

Large, open spaces, for instance, are most appropriate for practicing locomotor skills and for movement involving props (whether ribbon sticks or playground balls). A smooth, flat surface is best for games like jump rope and hopscotch, while a smooth, grassy surface lends itself to running and playing tag. Young children also love walking and running up and down hills and to practice walking on curbs or the edge of a sandbox. Both of these activities enhance balancing skills. And the school or public playground is generally the best place to practice hanging and swinging on the monkey bars, climbing up and gliding down a slide, or maneuvering a seesaw.

As far as feedback is concerned, the most important thing you can remember is to keep it neutral and encouraging. We too often believe we need to tell children what they've done wrong—so they can fix it. But if you do need to make corrections, keep the "sandwich" approach in mind. First, compliment the child on something she's done right. Then suggest a way to eliminate the error. Finally, end with something positive, even if it's to reiterate the first point.

To be truly helpful to a child, movement and physical education specialists are cautioned against "moralizing" with their feedback. Parents can benefit from the same advice. A jump isn't "good" or "bad." A jump is either high or low, light or heavy. If we use the former descriptors—or use such general terms as "good job," "good girl/boy," or "I liked that jump"—we aren't really telling the child anything. He has no idea what was "good" about what he did. But if we *describe* what we've seen ("You landed very lightly from your jump, with your knees bent. That helps keep your knees from getting hurt."), we not only provide vocabulary for what he's done; we provide useful specifics as well.

Also, when offering feedback, make sure it's meaningful to the child. For example, young children have no way to understand comments about the velocity of a throw. They do understand what *slow* and *fast* mean. If a child doesn't change the way she does something after receiving feedback from you, offer it again but with different words.

Finally, when providing feedback, make sure you give it in small amounts. Young children can generally absorb only one bit of information at a time. So, if your child is practicing his long jump and you're instructing him to "swing your arms out and up and extend your knees and hips on takeoff; then bring your arms back down and bend your knees in preparation for landing," he'll likely miss most—if not all—of the information!

Following are some activities that use locomotor skills:

- **In and Around.** There's nothing like an obstacle course to provide practice with any number of skills, including crawling, creeping, walking, and jumping. Additionally, an obstacle course will offer your child valuable experience with prepositions such as *over, under, around,* and *through.* Depending on your child's level of development (you can even use obstacle courses with babies who are only creeping), set up a course using large empty boxes to move through, chairs or other pieces of furniture big enough to move under, jump ropes to move over, or small items to move around. Then lead your child through the maze. Every time you play this game, you can arrange the objects differently and even give them different purposes. For instance, if the jump rope was originally lying on the floor for leaping or jumping over, you can later suspend it between two pieces of furniture for creeping under.

- **Chasing Bubbles.** Want to give children a reason to run and jump? Take them outside and invite them to catch the bubbles you blow! They'll let you know when they're tired—but until then, keep on blowing.

- **Jump!** Place your child on the bottom of a set of steps—or on the edge of a low sandbox or a curb, for instance—and stand facing her. Hold out your arms and encourage her to jump. Repeat the process as long as she stays interested. When she's ready for something a bit higher, use a sturdy plastic crate or something similar.

- **Ring-Around-the-Rosy.** If there are at least three people available (two children and an adult), play this traditional game for practice with sliding—and sitting. It also offers experience with the spatial concepts of *around* and *down*.

- **Follow the Leader.** This game offers a great opportunity for practice of various motor skills. Even if it's just you and your child, the game is plenty of fun. Just lead the way around the living room or backyard, performing as many different locomotor skills as you know your child can replicate. Don't forget to vary your movements with the elements of movement, changing direction, level, pathway, speed, force, and body shape. And you can incorporate both bound flow and nonlocomotor skills into the game by occasionally stopping and performing, say, a stretch, bend, twist, or shake.

- **Traffic Lights.** For this game you'll need three large pieces of paper or cardboard—one red, one green, and one yellow. When you hold up the green paper, the children walk. (You can play this game with one or several children.) When you hold up the yellow, they walk in place. At the sight of the red, they stop and wait. Start with walking until they get the hang of it. Then play it with any other locomotor skills they can perform.

- **In and Out.** Place one plastic hoop per child on the floor or ground. Then invite the children to jump in and out of the hoop, all the way around. When the children are able to hop, invite them to hop in and out. (The best way to help your child learn to hop is to hold his hand and hop right alongside him.)

- **Tag with a Twist.** A game of tag is a great way to get children to practice both running and dodging. To be sure the latter is involved, gradually reduce the available area in which the children can play.

Now, here are some activities involving manipulative skills:

- **Throwing.** Infants love to throw, so you'll want to give them plenty of soft items with which to practice. With an older child, as mentioned, accuracy isn't the first objective in teaching this skill. Rather, a child must initially become familiar with the throwing action itself. You can begin by providing foam or yarn balls and challenging her to practice throwing them at a wall (a target that's hard to miss!). When she's ready for a greater challenge, ask her to throw at a large target, like a hoop hung on the wall. She can also practice throwing beanbags or balls into a large box or a rubber trash barrel. As your child becomes more proficient, decrease the size of the targets.

- **Ball Rolling.** Even babies can roll and receive a large ball. You and your little one should be seated, legs straddled, and facing each other. Roll the ball to her and encourage her to push it back to you. Later, ask her to roll balls of various sizes at a wall. Once she's comfortable with this, try bowling with a large ball and empty soda bottles. Gradually you can decrease the size of the ball.

- **Volleying.** This action involves striking an object in an upward direction with the hands or other body parts (excluding the feet). When working with a young child, start with a lightweight, colorful object like a balloon to ensure success. Invite him first to hit the balloon upward and forward with both hands. The next step is to volley the balloon with just one (the dominant) hand, later trying it with the nondominant hand. Finally, challenge him to volley the balloon with different body parts. How many can he volley with?

- **Bouncing.** Begin with a large playground ball or a small beach ball, which the child initially bounces and catches with two hands, varying the number of bounces between catches. Once she's comfortable with this, challenge her to bounce continuously with two hands. The final challenge is to bounce with one (the dominant) hand, eventually bouncing with the nondominant hand as well. (Remember: there will probably be as much chasing as bouncing in the beginning.)

- **Striking.** A good rule for exploring this skill is, at first, the object and the child should be stationary, as when a child strikes a large ball off a cone or tee with a large plastic bat. Next the object moves, but the child remains still (as when the child hits a pitched beach ball with a paddle

Locomotion!

Following are descriptions of the basic locomotor skills. Following the principle of "fundamentals first," you want to be sure your child acquires the ability to execute these important movements. The descriptions, adapted from *Experiences in Movement* by Rae Pica, will help ensure they learn to execute them well.

You should know that this list represents a *general* developmental progression of locomotor skills. If you look through a dozen motor development texts, you'll rarely find unanimous agreement among authors as to the exact order in which children acquire these skills. So there's no need to worry if, for example, your child gallops before she jumps.

- **Crawl.** Lying on the stomach, with head and shoulders raised off the floor and the weight of the upper torso supported by the elbows. Locomotion involves moving the elbows and hips.

- **Creep.** Requires using the hands and knees or hands and feet to move the body through space and is the child's first efficient form of locomotion.

- **Walk.** Moves the body through space by transferring weight from the ball and toes of one foot to the heel of the other. Continual contact is made with the floor. Limbs are used in opposition.

- **Run.** Transfers the body's weight from the ball and toes of one foot to the ball and toes of the other. The body should be inclined forward slightly, and the arms should be bent slightly, swinging in opposition to the legs.

- **Jump.** Propels the body upward from a takeoff on one or both feet. The toes, which are the last part of the foot to leave the ground (heel-ball-toe), are the first to reach it on landing, with landings occurring on both feet (toe-ball-heel). Knees should bend to absorb the shock of landing.

- **Leap.** Similar to a run, except the knee and ankle action is greater. The knee leads following the takeoff and is then extended as the foot reaches forward to land. The back leg extends to the rear while in the air, but once the front foot has landed, the rear leg swings forward into the next lift.

- **Gallop.** Performed with an uneven rhythm, it is a combination of a walk and a run in which one foot leads and the other plays catch-up. Children will lead with the preferred foot long before they feel comfortable leading with the other foot.

- **Hop.** Propels the body upward from a takeoff on one foot (heel-ball-toe). The landing is made on the same foot (toe-ball-heel). The free leg doesn't touch the ground.

- **Slide.** A gallop performed sideways. One foot leads and the other plays catch-up, and the uneven rhythm remains the same as in the gallop. Because facing one direction and moving in another is difficult for young children, they'll learn to slide much later than they learn to gallop.

- **Skip.** A combination of a step and a hop, the skip, like the gallop and the slide, has an uneven rhythm. With more emphasis placed on the hop than the step, the overall effect is of a light, skimming motion during which the feet only momentarily leave the ground. The lead foot alternates. For many children skipping initially on one side only is a normal developmental stage.

---

or large, lightweight bat). The final challenge occurs when the object and the child both move (for example, keeping a ball in the air with a paddle).

- **Dribbling.** In the context of this book, *dribbling* refers to the manipulation of an object with the feet. A child should first practice dribbling with a beanbag, which is considerably less dynamic than a ball. Later, using a small beach ball or a playground ball eight to twelve inches in diameter, the child can begin controlling the ball with the inside and outside of his feet. Once he's able to do this successfully, provide a pathway (for instance, with two long jump ropes lying parallel on the ground)—and later an obstacle course—for him to dribble through. Encourage him to alternate feet!

6

Promoting Your Child's Fitness

"We are raising the first generation of children who are less healthy than their parents."

—KEITH GEIGER, PRESIDENT
NATIONAL EDUCATION ASSOCIATION

EVERYBODY WANTS TO BE physically fit. We associate fitness with good health and probably carry an image in our minds of what it looks like to be fit: trim, well toned, and sporting a vital "glow." But what, exactly, is physical fitness? How do the experts define it?

In specific terms physical fitness consists of two components: health-related fitness and skill-related fitness. The former, which is described in greater detail in the next section, includes cardiovascular endurance, muscular strength, muscular endurance, flexibility, and body composition. Skill-related fitness incorporates balance, agility, coordination, power, speed, and reaction time.

Defining it more generally, the President's Council on Physical Fitness and Sports says physical fitness is:

> the ability to perform daily tasks vigorously and alertly, with energy left over for enjoying leisure-time activities and meeting emergency demands. It is the ability to endure, to bear up, to withstand stress, to carry on in circumstances where an unfit person could not continue, and is a major basis for good health and well-being.

The American Alliance for Health, Physical Education, Recreation and Dance (AAHPERD) states simply that physical fitness is:

> a physical state of well-being that allows people to (1) perform daily activities with vigor, (2) reduce their risk of health problems relative to lack of exercise, and (3) establish a fitness base for participation in a variety of physical activities.

Given these definitions, you'd probably say yes if asked if you'd like to be physically fit. And certainly you'd want the same for your child. But the problem is not in the wanting; it's in the getting—and what people are and are not willing to do for it.

As you might imagine, physical fitness is a personal matter; it differs from one individual to another. That's because it's subject to a number of factors. Some, like gender, age, and heredity, can't be changed. (According to a study of four thousand families conducted by York University in Ontario, we inherit at least 50 percent of our flexibility, strength, endurance, and speed from our parents because characteristics such as blood volume, muscle development, and heart size are determined genetically.) Others, including personal habits, diet, and physical activity levels, can and do impact fitness but require effort on the part of the individual.

One thing we know for sure about physical fitness is that it's fleeting. It can't be maintained without continuing attention to it. This is particularly relevant where our children are concerned. Although research has yet to show a direct link between physical activity and physical fitness in children, we do know that, in general, the latter isn't possible without the former. The more active children are—and stay—the more likely they are to be fit.

If your child is to achieve quality of life in terms of health, he—and you—will have to learn to make the most of those elements that can't be changed and to make an effort with regard to those that can be. You'll need to understand that, especially where children are concerned, fitness is an ongoing *process*, not a product to be obtained once and for all. Perhaps most important, if this process is to succeed, you should realize you can't apply adult concepts of physical fitness and exercise to children.

But before we get to all that, let's look more closely at what health-related fitness entails.

The Five Fitness Factors

If you're going to help your child along the path to fitness, it's important to have some understanding of the components involved. It's also important that you realize, in early childhood, that the emphasis should be placed on the health-related, as opposed to the skill-related, components of fitness. So that's what we'll talk about here.

Cardiovascular Endurance

Cardiovascular endurance is the ability of the heart and lungs to supply oxygen and nutrients to the muscles. In simple terms someone with great cardiovascular endurance has a strong heart—one that actually grows in size and pumps more blood with every beat, resulting in a lower heart rate. As you can imagine, this can happen only when an individual exercises regularly. Typically it's aerobic exercise that improves cardiovascular fitness, but where children are concerned we can't think of "aerobics" in the same way that we do for adults.

As you'll read later, young children are not made for long, uninterrupted periods of strenuous activity. So expecting them to jog, walk briskly, or follow an exercise video for twenty to thirty minutes, particularly before the age of six, is not only unrealistic but could be damaging. (At the very least it can ensure an intense dislike of physical activity.) Rather, when we consider developmentally appropriate aerobic activities for children, we should be thinking along the lines of moderate to vigorous play and movement. (Physical activity that's moderately intense will increase the heart rate and breathing somewhat, while vigorous-intensity movement takes a lot more effort and will result in a noticeable increase in breathing. The latter can usually be sustained for a maximum of twenty to thirty minutes.) Riding a bicycle, swimming, walking, marching, playing tag, dancing to moderate- to fast-paced music, and jumping rope all fall under the heading of moderate- to vigorous-intensity exercise for children. In other words it's anything that keeps the child moving continuously, sometimes strenuously and sometimes less so.

The American Heart Association assures us we needn't be concerned with target heart rates in children. Yes, we want to get their hearts pump-

What About Fitness Testing?

If your child is, or will be, enrolled in an elementary school that offers physical education, chances are she'll eventually have to undergo fitness testing. Is that a good thing? Here's some information to help you decide.

As with most things in life, there are pros and cons to fitness testing. On the positive side, it now focuses on the health-related components of fitness rather than athletic and motor skill, as it did in the past. And it does provide an opportunity for you and your child to determine his relative strengths and weaknesses and to chart progress—or lack thereof—from year to year.

But there are a number of pitfalls concerning fitness testing:

- These tests tend to compare children of the same age. But since children develop at different rates, the comparison isn't necessarily fair.
- Many fitness tests require children to perform until they simply can't any longer, and that can only create distaste for movement in all but the most motivated of children.
- Studies have shown that children consider fitness test items the least fun activities in physical education class. And, since certain activities were designated specifically for fitness, children failed to recognize that the activities they enjoy also contribute to fitness.
- Fitness test scores are determined to a large degree by genetics and rate of maturity, so ranking children against one another is a questionable process.

Additionally, Judith A. Flohr and Jacqueline A. Williams, writing in a 1997 article in *The Physical Educator*, report that young children often don't see the relevance of fitness testing. They state: "If a physical education teacher conveys to his/her students that a strong relationship exists between fitness test scores and activity and the child fails to meet the test expectations, . . . the child may be discouraged from continued participation in fitness and fitness testing."

If your child is required to undergo fitness testing at school, make it a point to learn how it's handled and what the physical education teacher's attitude toward it is. If you're not satisfied with the process or the philosophy (for example, if test scores are posted for all to see, which should never be the case), you'll need to have a heart-to-heart with your child. Reassure her that her level of activity, rather than test scores, is a better gauge of real fitness.

ing on a daily basis, but whenever possible we want to ensure it happens naturally. If you've noticed your child is definitely not getting enough exercise to improve cardiovascular fitness, joining in on the play yourself may be all that's needed. Start slowly, gradually increasing the length of time you maintain movement (by a few minutes a week) and stopping immediately should your child experience any discomfort. Before you know it, daily or almost-daily, moderate- to vigorous-intensity activity will be a way of life.

Muscular Strength

Muscular strength is fairly self-explanatory but is described as the ability to exert force with a single maximum effort. Strong muscles are necessary not only for performing certain tasks, like throwing for distance, hanging and swinging, climbing, and carrying heavy books and groceries, but also for preventing injury and maintaining proper posture. An added bonus is that increasing muscle strength also increases strength in tendons, ligaments, and bones.

Strength training—also known as resistance or weight training—is the best way to build muscular strength. But here again, we must view things differently than if we were discussing adults. While there's a lot of debate over the appropriateness of involving young children in strength training, there are some points on which the experts agree.

First, it's never a good idea to modify an adult strength-training program for children. Adults' bodies are fully developed; children's are not. Adults have long attention spans and the motivation to endure the monotony of repetitive exercises; children do not. For these reasons the best "strength training" for children involves the use of their own weight in physical activities they'd be performing anyway, like jumping, playing tug-of-war, and pumping higher and higher on a swing.

Recently a photograph accompanying a *Denver Post* article about children's fitness programs showed what looked to be a three-year-old girl doing an overhead press (in poor form, it should be added) with a special "children's" barbell. The instructors quoted spoke enthusiastically about the need for appropriate child-sized equipment. But here, too, most experts agree: Children under the age of eight shouldn't be using weights or machines—child-sized or not. The general rule of thumb is that only children mature enough to follow specific instructions and understand the risks and benefits of such training should be handling strength-training equipment. Dr. Kenneth Cooper recommends children wait until they're ten—preferably twelve—to use apparatus. He worries that before puberty children may not have the judgment necessary to use it safely.

There's a good deal of interest in children's fitness right now and plenty of programs cropping up to take advantage of that interest. These programs will heartily endorse the benefits of strength training, convincing parents that it will prevent their children from injury and improve their sports skills. And, yes, if children are participating in organized sports without the requisite strength, strength-*related* activities *may* help prevent sports-related injuries. But strength training, handled improperly, can do more harm than good, particularly in children under six, who are most prone to injury. And the truth is, the best way for children to improve their sports skills is to learn and practice their specific sports skills.

According to Nancy E. Sayre and Jere Dee Gallagher, authors of *The Young Child and the Environment*, strength isn't a factor in movement and sport for the young child. Skill level, they contend, makes the difference.

If you're considering the pros and cons of strength training, here are some things you should know:

- Children should always begin by using the resistance of their own body weight. In addition to the examples cited earlier, this could include such formal exercises as heel raises, curl-ups, leg lifts, and wall push-ups.

- If your older (six- to eight-year-old) child is going to participate in some sort of formal regimen, that regimen should include a warm-up (for example, jogging in place to circulate blood throughout the body) and a cooldown (gentle stretches held for ten to twelve seconds). Stretching shouldn't be used as a warm-up, because "cold" muscles shouldn't be stretched.

- Once children do begin to use apparatus, they should do so without any added weight or resistance. When a child can perform eight to fifteen repetitions of an exercise, weight can be added in *small* increments. Children should never lift the maximal weight!

- A knowledgeable adult should constantly monitor children participating in strength-training programs.

- Children benefit more from additional repetitions of moderate weight than from fewer repetitions of heavy weights.

- Strength training may further elevate the blood pressure in children with hypertension.

- The National Strength and Conditioning Association cites improper training techniques, lifting heavy or maximal weights, improper equipment, and lack of qualified adult supervision as the most common reasons for injuries.

The American Academy of Pediatrics states that gains in strength, muscle size, and power are lost after only six weeks once strength training is stopped. So, if your child is to improve muscular strength, "strength training" must be continuous. And, honestly, the only way that's going to happen for young children is if it's part of what they naturally do—and it's fun.

Muscular Endurance

Muscular endurance is the muscles' ability to continue contracting over an extended period of time. In other words, it's about stamina. Write Joanne Landy and Keith Burridge, in *50 Simple Things You Can Do to Raise a Child Who Is Physically Fit*: "Good muscular endurance gives you the ability to repeat a movement without getting tired or to hold a position or carry something for a long period of time without being fatigued. A child who has good muscular endurance will enjoy and have greater success in his/her daily work activities, in play, and in sporting and athletic competitions."

Obviously muscular endurance is tied to muscular strength; so many of the same kinds of activities and exercises benefit both. However, muscular endurance also depends on skill level. A skilled individual has the ability to perform movements in the most efficient manner; it comes naturally to him after years of practice. That means he can sustain movement for lengthier periods of time. A child, by virtue of having fewer years of practice in most skills, will use the maximum force and contract more muscles than actually needed for the movement. Therefore, she won't be able to last as long as a skilled mover.

Flexibility

Flexibility is the range of motion around joints. When people possess good flexibility, they can stretch to put something on a high shelf, bend to tie a shoe, or sit cross-legged without effort or aches and pains. They can swing a tennis racket or a golf club, perform a layup in basketball, or reach for a high fly without fear of muscle strain, sprain, or spasm.

In general, girls tend to be more flexible than boys, who start to lose their flexibility at around age ten. Girls begin to lose flexibility at twelve. But this doesn't have to happen. If children are physically active, they'll be flexible. But they should also be encouraged to work on their flexibility through gentle, static stretches that take a muscle just beyond its usual length (without pain!) and are held for at least ten seconds.

Two no-nos regarding stretching: First, children should work their own limbs through their range of motion; it's extremely easy for an adult to stretch a child's muscles and joints too far. Second, children should be warned against ballistic (bouncing) stretching. It can cause small tears in the muscle fibers and is not as effective as static stretching. (Have you ever wondered why professional football players are constantly getting injured? One reason may be that nobody seems to have warned them of the dangers of ballistic stretching; you can see them every Sunday during football season, on the sidelines, bouncing away.)

Which brings us to a final point about flexibility: it doesn't have to be limited by greater muscle strength. We may not typically associate flexibility with those in the big-muscle set, like football players and bodybuilders. But the big muscles aren't the problem; lack of proper stretching is.

Body Composition

The final component of health-related fitness is body composition: the body's makeup in terms of fat, muscle, tissue, and bone or the percentage of lean body tissue to fat.

Obviously, with childhood obesity becoming more of a problem as the years go by, a lot of attention is focused on body composition right now. But weight alone is not a good indicator of body composition. Some children are simply large-boned. Also, muscle weighs more than fat. So it's possible for two children to have the same weight but very different makeups, one possessing very little fat and the other too much.

Generally you can tell if your child has too much body fat. But if you want to know for sure, there are a number of professionals, including nutritionists, physical education teachers, and certified exercise specialists at health clubs, who are qualified to take body fat measurements. If you're unsure where to go, consult your pediatrician. The Centers for Disease Control have also created growth charts that can help you determine your child's body mass index (BMI). You can find them online at cdc.gov/growth charts.

Physical activity, of course, is the key to combating body fat, with aerobic and muscle-strengthening movement offering the most bang for the buck. Research shows that inactive preschool children were almost four times more likely to enter first grade with increased body fatness. By ensuring our children stay active, we can combat obesity *before* it starts rather than once it's upon them!

We're Not Talking Richard Simmons Here

Of course it's important to have all this information. But, as the parent of a young child, you're probably wondering what to do with it. Should you start creating a fitness plan for your child? Should you enroll him in an organized program? Is there something you can run out and buy that will help?

As mentioned in the introduction of this chapter, success will come only if you accept the fact that you can't apply adult concepts of physical fitness and exercise to children. So, if you're envisioning some kind of regularly scheduled program of cardiovascular and strength-training exercises to do on a weekly basis with your child, think again. That will seem more like yucky-tasting medicine to a kid than fun—and, unless it's fun, she won't be interested. Also, children won't exercise for the same reasons we adults do.

Most adults exercise for the sake of their health or because they want to look good. Children should *never* be encouraged to exercise because it will make them look good, even if obesity is an issue. Emphasizing exercise for the sake of appearance places the wrong value on physical activity—and appearance! Body image issues are especially important to keep in mind where young girls are concerned. According to a 1991 study of more than a thousand first- through third-grade girls, 42 percent of them already preferred body shapes different from and thinner than their own!

Besides, the last thing we want to do is label a child. A child who grows up thinking he's "chubby," for instance, will likely think of himself that way throughout his life, regardless of how his body changes.

As far as health benefits are concerned, unlike adults, young children live very much in the present moment. They're simply incapable of projecting themselves into the future. So you can't expect your toddler, preschooler, or even your first- or second-grader to exercise because it will ensure he's healthier at age forty or he'll look and feel better at sixty. Even if you explain that exercise will make him healthier *right now*, you're not likely to get an enthusiastic response. These are all adult concepts—adult goals—beyond a child's cognitive and emotional capabilities.

And you know what? Even if you could convince your child of the need for daily or three-times-a-week exercise and you were right there alongside her, working up a sweat and the two of you "into shape," any results achieved would most probably be temporary. If physical activity is something your child has had imposed on her, she's likely to stop doing it as soon as the choice is hers to make. Then any benefits gained will soon be lost. As mentioned, fitness is fleeting.

Even if you reward your child for time spent in physical activity—with stickers or coins or much-desired TV or computer time—what happens when there are no longer rewards forthcoming? When the child has grown up, is on his own, and there's no immediate payoff for dragging himself out of bed half an hour early or for hitting the road for a jog after a long day in class or at work?

The goal is to ensure lifelong fitness. That means your child will have to grow up with a love of physical activity and the way it makes her feel.

An article entitled "Intrinsic Motivation in Sports and Exercise" (at fitness.gov) reports on two studies that make excellent points. In the first, adult women who'd recently joined a health club met with instructors to discuss their activity preferences. They were then randomly placed in one of two groups: one with perceived choice and one with perceived lack of choice. Although the activities assigned to them were actually those they'd said they preferred, the women in the so-called no-choice group thought their instructor had determined their activities. Six weeks later the women in the perceived-choice group had higher attendance and expressed greater intent to continue their enrollment.

The second study looked at the effect of rewarding children to play on a piece of popular equipment: the balance board. The researchers' hypothesis was that a trophy (an extrinsic reward) for performing on the balance board would be perceived by the children as controlling. And, sure enough, the children who'd been rewarded trophies were later less inclined to play on the board during free-choice times than those who'd expected no rewards.

The morals: when individuals, whether children or adults, do something that's not their choice, they're less willing to do it. And when they do something for a reward, they're likely to stop doing it once the reward is no longer available. Rewards and recognition also promote a product-oriented view of fitness. Once received, the process is finished.

So, what about organized fitness programs for children? Will they motivate children to move?

A quick Internet search shows there are plenty of people—and franchises—willing to offer their solutions to your child's fitness problems. You can take your child to classes at the local YMCA or YWCA or to one of the many health clubs now offering programs for kids as well as adults. Or you can enroll your child at one of the Gymboree, Little Gym, or My Gym franchises cropping up in more and more cities and towns.

On the positive side, these organizations offer children—and parents—opportunities for socialization as well as physical activity. And, as long as the activities are developmentally appropriate (e.g., no overhead presses for three-year-olds), facilitated by trained instructors with knowledge of early childhood, and *fun*, they provide yet another chance for children to move and to love it.

But there are a couple of cautions. First, if you're expecting one of these programs to make a superstar athlete out of your child, you'll have to dial back your expectations. They won't provide an advantage any more than earlier-is-better infant programs or enrollment in organized sports (as we've covered in previous chapters).

Also, Dr. Jorge Gomez, a member of the AAP Committee on Sports Medicine and Fitness, worries that parents are being led to believe that taking their children to a gym three times a week and letting someone else train them is somehow equivalent to spending quality time with them. The best programs are going to be those that involve child and parent together.

You additionally want to consider whether or not going to one of these programs is your child's choice. Again, if you're imposing it on him, physical activity in general could come to leave a bad taste in his mouth. And does the program offer rewards at the end of each exercise or session, reinforcing extrinsic motivation?

Finally, there's the very real possibility that your child will come to think of physical activity and fitness as things you have to go *elsewhere* to get. And, since lives tend to get busier rather than more leisurely, as children get older and grow into adults, the possibility also exists that eventually there won't be enough time to go elsewhere, like to a gym or health club. We want our children to know they don't have to go out of their way to move!

For most of us finding the time, energy, and motivation to exercise is difficult, to say the least. As adults we may be counting on certain rewards like fitting into something worn years before or just the guilt-free "permission" to eat dessert once a week. But still, much of our incentive comes from inside ourselves. For children, unless there's intrinsic motivation, there's no good reason to do anything—in the present moment, throughout childhood, or into adulthood. And just as it does for adults, intrinsic motivation for children comes from feeling good about something.

What constitutes intrinsic motivation—feeling good—for children? As evidenced by the studies just cited, choice is certainly a major ingredient. Even the youngest children feel good when they get to make choices— when they're part of the decision-making process. In *Fit Kids!*, Kenneth Cooper contends that children involved in the process from the start are more likely to continue—even once an adult is no longer participating. So you'll want to include your child in any decisions made about how she— and the family—will be physically active.

A second factor contributing to intrinsic motivation for children is curiosity. As physical education specialist Curt Hinson writes in *Fitness for Children*: "When an activity arouses curiosity, a child becomes more motivated to partake for the sake of satisfying the curiosity. The curious child participates for her or his own reasons, not yours." (Would your child be curious about what happens to his heartbeat after a run around the yard—or about how many sounds he can hear in a walk around the block?)

Developmentally appropriate activities that are neither too easy nor too difficult also help foster intrinsic motivation. Children become bored with activities that are too easy and frustrated by those that are too challenging.

Finally, to paraphrase the Cyndi Lauper song, kids just wanna have fun. What *really* feels good to children is having a good time! So rid yourself of those notions of pumping up, target heart rates, and "no pain, no gain" (not even a good idea for adults). Children's fitness demands a different approach. And, whenever possible, that approach should take the form of play. Think in terms of family fitness—quality time with your child that just happens to involve getting and staying physically fit—and you're on the road to health and happiness.

What's the Right Fitness "Plan" for Your Child?

Let's look first at the physical activity recommendations for adults, which have recently been revamped. It used to be that adults were advised to perform twenty to thirty minutes of aerobic activity—raising the heart rate to the appropriate level—at least three times a week. The new recommendations—approved by groups such as the Centers for Disease Control and Prevention, the National Institutes of Health, the American Heart Association, and the American College of Sports Medicine—now speak in terms of *accumulated* physical activity, at a moderate-intensity level, on most or all days of the week. In other words, these agencies are assuring us that ten- or fifteen-minute daily "bouts" of physical activity, adding up to thirty minutes, provide health benefits similar to those derived from one thirty-minute session. And, best of all, the activity doesn't have to be overly strenuous to be beneficial.

This is certainly good news for adults, especially those who've typically gotten little or no exercise. Suddenly fitness through physical activity seems more doable. But it's also good news that similar recommendations have been made for children, who were never equipped—physically, emotionally, or cognitively—to participate in strenuous, nonstop, thirty-minute physical activity sessions.

Children are naturally intermittent movers, so the idea of accumulating physical activity in bouts is perfect for them. They tire more easily than adults and so require frequent recovery periods, but they also recover more quickly than adults do. If you've ever watched them play, you've witnessed wonderfully alternating rhythms of inactivity and activity (some periods of low-intensity, some moderate-intensity, and some just plain all-out). They may run wildly for several minutes, then switch to skipping leisurely around the yard, followed by a period in which they're watching the progress of a caterpillar in the grass. Then they're ready to go again.

And, according to the experts, this is as it should be. The American Heart Association states: "Children are remarkably able to adjust their levels of activity to their individual capability." *The Surgeon General's Report on Physical Activity and Health* concurs, maintaining: "Young children do not perform many active tasks for sustained periods of time, so 30 minutes of continuous activity seems unlikely." And: "All people over the age of two years should accumulate at least 30 minutes of endurance-type physical activity, of at least moderate intensity, on most—preferably all—days of the week."

In 1998, the National Association for Sport and Physical Education (NASPE) published "Physical Activity for Children," guidelines for elementary-school children ages five to twelve. As this book is being written, those guidelines are being revised to emphasize the appropriateness of intermittent activity. The new guidelines will also recommend an accumulation of at least sixty minutes (up from thirty) of developmentally appropriate physical activity on all or most days of the week. (Sixty minutes is consistent with international standards.)

The guidelines additionally recommend that:

• Some of the child's activity each day be at moderate to vigorous levels, in periods lasting ten to fifteen minutes or more

- Children experience a *variety* of physical activities
- Extended periods of inactivity be discouraged

Consistent with these guidelines are those NASPE has published for children birth to five (see Appendix A). While it's recommended that infants simply be given opportunities to experience plenty of physical activity, toddlers and preschoolers are encouraged to accumulate at least thirty and sixty minutes, respectively, of structured physical activity and at least sixty minutes of unstructured physical activity per day. The guidelines state that neither group should be sedentary for more than sixty minutes at a time, except when sleeping. (This is also consistent with the surgeon general's recommendations for all children over the age of two.)

So, what does all of this mean, in terms of a fitness plan, for you and your child? Here, too, the experts agree. For young children the focus should be on the health-related, as opposed to the skill-related, components of physical fitness and on play rather than structured fitness programs or exercises. Following is advice from three major groups:

- The American Heart Association: "Emphasis should be placed on play (rather than exercise) and on activities the child enjoys, that are consistent with the child's skill level and that can be accomplished given the family's personal resources and interests." (Healthy children, they contend, will be active when in an environment conducive to physical activity.)

- The American Medical Association: "By encouraging even the youngest child to engage in active play, parents prompt a child's exploration and natural curiosity—how his body works."

- The American Academy of Pediatrics: "Free play designed to provide opportunities for each child to develop fundamental motor skills and to reach his or her potential at his or her own rate is preferable to structured sessions."

In other words, the "plan" should be that your child spend a good deal of time playing actively. You can use many of the activities described throughout this book to promote fitness. And sometimes all you need to do is insist your child play outdoors. Children who aren't allowed to hang around inside will find ways to keep themselves amused outside. Then those wonderfully alternating rhythms will naturally take over.

Of course all of these recommendations for free play don't mean you can't—or shouldn't—*plan* fitness activities for your child. Or, even better, for your child and you. But you may have to mentally adjust your definition of *fitness activities*.

Anything that gets you and your family moving counts toward fitness. And, although consistency is key to fitness, you don't have to rigidly maintain a Monday-Wednesday-Friday, same-time-of-day schedule. You may not want or be able to schedule a walk for the same time of day three days a week, but you can probably plan to sneak one in—or a bike ride or a frolic in the pool—a couple times a week. Then, if you make a game of parking as far away from the grocery store as you can, actively play with your child whenever possible, and schedule a family hike, a kite-flying session at the park, or a trip to the local bowling alley or skating rink on the weekend, you've successfully met or exceeded the experts' recommendations for time and energy expenditure! All this has the additional benefit of ensuring variety, which makes fitness more fun, uses different muscle groups, and helps your child discover what physical activities he likes best.

You can also include your child, in developmentally appropriate ways, in your own adult-style fitness activities. Thanks to backpacks, even the youngest child can "walk" or "run" along with you. And we've all seen those parents who walk or run while pushing a stroller or who ride a bike with a baby seat or baby trailer attached. Although the baby herself may not yet be reaping the benefits of the exercise, she's certainly forming early, positive impressions about exercise.

Susan Kalish, mother of two and author of *Your Child's Fitness*, talks about running while her son rode his bike alongside her. And when it was time for indoor aerobics, her preschool daughter simply danced along to the music on the tape.

All that heavy breathing may not seem like play to you, but it will to your child—because she's doing it with you. She'll also be learning, at an early age, to value physical activity—because you do.

The Truth About Trampolines

With about five hundred thousand trampolines sold for backyard use each year in the United States, the chances are good you've seen one in a yard near you. Perhaps you've witnessed a group of children happily bouncing away in a neighbor's yard and considered what a good tool it would be, for both keeping children active and promoting fitness. After all, the exercise would specifically benefit cardiovascular endurance and muscular strength, and the children certainly looked like they were having fun!

Then it might surprise you to learn that the American Academy of Pediatrics (AAP) made the following recommendations in a 1999 policy statement:

1. Parents should never purchase a home trampoline or allow children to use home trampolines.
2. The trampoline should not be part of routine physical education classes in schools.
3. The trampoline has no place in outdoor playgrounds and should never be regarded as play equipment.

The reason for the strong stance? In 1996 approximately 83,400 trampoline-related injuries occurred in the United States—140 percent more than were reported in 1990. (In 1998 the Consumer Product Safety Commission estimated that ninety-five thousand trampoline-related injuries had been treated in hospital emergency rooms.) The majority of these injuries happened on home tramps, with the greatest percentage of the injured children ages five to fourteen. Children under age five had the second-highest rate of injury. From 1990 to the time of the AAP policy statement in May 1999, there were six deaths involving trampolines, most from falls.

Given these statistics, if you were considering buying a backyard trampoline, you might want to decide against it. And you certainly don't want to allow your child to play on a trampoline in someone else's yard.

But what if you already own one and feel strongly about keeping it? The Consumer Product Safety Commission offers these tips to help prevent serious injuries:

- Allow only one person on the trampoline at a time.
- Do not attempt or allow somersaults.
- Do not allow a trampoline to be used without shock-absorbing pads that completely cover the springs, hooks, and frame.

- Place the trampoline away from structures and other play areas. Use shock-absorbent materials on the ground around the perimeter.
- Do not use a ladder with the trampoline, because it provides unsupervised access by small children. No child under six years of age should use a regular-size trampoline. Secure the trampoline to prevent unauthorized and unattended use.
- Always supervise children who use a trampoline.

Developing the Fitness Habit

Once again: fitness is fleeting. While most children are born healthy and fit, not all of them remain that way. According to Curt Hinson, doing so depends in great part on four factors: environment, attitude, knowledge, and lifestyle. All of these elements are within your control. Let's look at them one at a time.

Environment

What does your child's environment consist of? When forced to stay indoors due to inclement weather, is his only choice to sit still somewhere? Or is there room for the two of you to put on a CD and dance? To play Twister? Or perhaps even to twirl hula hoops around your waists and other body parts? Is there somewhere in the house where space for activity is valued more than the display of easily broken knickknacks?

What about the outdoor environment? Does it include open areas for running, jumping, rolling, and the like? Is there a tree or purchased equipment for safe climbing, hanging, and swinging? How about a sandbox so your toddler can dig and haul? Does your child have access to activity-oriented toys, like a tricycle or bicycle, balls, or ribbon sticks, like the ones the rhythmic gymnasts use?

Attitude

Setting up the environment for physical activity also falls under the heading of demonstrating a proper attitude, as does exhibiting enjoyment toward physical activity. Do you moan and groan when it's "time" to put in the aerobics tape? Do you get off your bike or finish your walk huffing and puffing and making it seem like an ordeal? Or do you express enthusiasm as you lace up your sneakers or following a brisk stroll? It's OK if children understand that sometimes physical activity is an effort as long as they also understand that anything worth doing is worth some effort.

Most important, do you play with your child? There's research showing that the influence of parents and siblings does indeed increase children's physical activity levels. In fact your actual participation in your child's activities (especially if he's in the under-seven set) will have much more effect on his activity levels than if you simply insist he be active.

Children learn by watching you. If you spend the majority of your free time in sedentary activities, like watching television, that's what they'll want to do, too. But if you spend your free time playing, not only will they have someone to play with, they'll have a terrific role model. Because you have a playful, positive attitude toward physical activity, they'll assume the same.

Knowledge

Knowledge comes into play when you help your child understand why you and she take part in physical activity—why it's necessary (which will help ensure that a positive attitude toward fitness endures beyond childhood). Certainly lecturing children on the topic isn't likely to have much of an impact; you'll make the greatest impression mostly by example. But you can also offer a well-placed word or two. For example, as you stretch out: "It's important to stretch after exercising so your muscles don't get all bunched up." Or, to stimulate your child's natural curiosity: "Wow—chasing bubbles really got my heart pumping. It's healthy to do that sometimes. Is yours going faster, too?"

Your child should also know why you choose family activities like skating, swimming, and roller blading ("It's important to be active so we can be healthy"). And she should have a vote as you decide on the family's adventures. Would she rather go for a walk or a bike ride? Would she prefer going to the playground to mess around on the equipment or playing Frisbee in the park? Remember: choice is a necessary ingredient in fostering intrinsic motivation.

Lifestyle

Finally, there's lifestyle. If your child is to derive the benefits of physical fitness, then physical activity must be habitual and lifelong. *Moving* should be as routine as brushing teeth and bathing.

A Harvard study conducted in 2000 demonstrated that children regularly overestimate the amount of time they spend moving. When outlining their activities for the day before, the forty-five participants (eleven to thirteen years old) reported an hour of vigorous exercise, like running. But they'd been wearing motion recorders on their hips that exposed the truth of the matter: they'd actually engaged in vigorous activity for *two minutes*. The hours of the day not spent in school (ten, on average) had been spent in sedentary activity, like playing videos, watching TV, and sleeping.

When physical activity becomes habitual, this sort of delusion isn't likely to occur. And, if we're to instill habits, not surprisingly, early childhood is the best time to start.

Kenneth Cooper, in *Fit Kids!*, suggests that one way to help make physical activity routine is to use a wall chart listing your child's fitness activities in colored pencils or crayons. You then place a star or an animal sticker next to each activity completed. (You'll have to emphasize that this is simply a way of keeping track, as opposed to granting rewards.) Or you could simply create awareness with words, reminding children when they haven't had enough movement and responding enthusiastically when they have.

All the suggestions made in the previous paragraphs and in the previous section will help you instill the fitness habit in your child. Most important, if physical activity is a habit of yours—and of your family's—it will become a habit of his. And it will be an easy one to keep if it's associated with pleasure rather than pain.

A pleasant association is most likely to happen if you:

- Choose individual and family activities that fit easily into your lifestyle.
- Select activities that are within your physical capabilities and those of your family members.
- Pace activities with fun, rather than heart rates, in mind.

- Don't worry about scheduling; consistency is important, but it's OK to be flexible.
- Encourage one another, pointing out what's *right* about what you're seeing.
- Don't insist a child do something she's not comfortable with; you can always try again in several months.
- Expose your child to a wide variety of physical experiences. Just as you wouldn't feed your child only chicken and spinach, you shouldn't limit activity choices.
- Keep competition out of the equation. No good can come from comparing children.

It's important, too, to view fitness as an ongoing process rather than as a product. The latter gives the impression that there's an end point to be reached, which is a misconception and can create discouragement. It's also a great idea for your child to know that it's a process for you, too! If she believes you've achieved some ideal standards, she'll seek to reach perfection herself; and just the idea of perfection can prove to be overwhelming and not worth attempting. On the other hand, if she's aware of your shortcomings (and we all have them), she'll be motivated by your continuing commitment to improving.

Writes Curt Hinson, in *Fitness for Children*: "Your goal should be to teach children that their level is acceptable, wherever they are on the continuum, while at the same time encouraging them to move in a positive direction."

Finally, with regard to lifestyle: chores count, too. A July 2000 *Time* article informs that a ninety-pound person who washes dishes for five minutes burns four more calories than if he or she was watching TV for the same amount of time. Carrying groceries up stairs burns twenty-seven calories. Yes, you want to emphasize play. But you also want responsible children, and responsible children take on their share of chores. When those chores include raking the leaves, sweeping the floor, or walking the dog, children become not only responsible but also more fit.

The goal is to make physical activity a customary part of your child's—and your—life. However you choose to encourage the physical activity habit, you can be assured that if it's introduced early in life, your child won't be among those who only *think* they get enough activity during the day.

What's a Parent to Do?

Much of this chapter has been devoted to what a parent can do to promote a child's fitness. Following are some additional suggestions.

- Although rewarding physical activity isn't a good idea, using physical activity as a reward is. For example, you might suggest a family hike or a trip to a nearby lake as a reward at the end of a long week. Thinking of physical activity as a reward gives it the right spin.

- Buy movement-oriented toys. If your child has more active than sedentary toys, it will limit his choices in a good way. When it's time for gift giving, select items like hula hoops; balls in a variety of shapes, sizes, and textures; roller skates; a jump rope; juggling scarves; a shovel and pail; a little red wagon; or a wading pool or swing set. When shopping for games, Twister has more to offer than Chutes and Ladders. And CDs with lively music are a better choice than movie videos.

- Limit TV time and don't allow a set in the bedroom.

- Don't make a walk or a jog about exercise only. You can use this time to strengthen the bond with your child by talking to her as you stroll together. Let her choose the topic! She'll be thrilled by your undivided attention.

- Get creative! Exercise doesn't have to be a bore—and it shouldn't be if you want your child to learn to love it. If you're stuck inside and your little one hasn't had enough movement, put a lively march on the CD player and hold a "parade" around the living room. To introduce your toddler or preschooler to stretching, pretend to be reaching for something on a high shelf, shooting a basketball, climbing a ladder, or trying to pluck a star from the sky. Play a game of point and flex, where you sit facing each other with legs straddled, alternately pointing your toes toward each other and then aiming them toward the ceiling, holding in each position for a second or two. Make up a song about pointing and flexing! Turn tedious heel raises and knee bends into a game of popcorn, where you and your child stand and alternately lift your heels, lower them, and then bend and straighten your knees, pretending to be popcorn popping. Make the sounds that go with it!

If the way to promote motor development is to practice, practice, practice, then the way to get your child on the road to physical fitness is to model, model, model. As busy as you may be, if you truly want physical fitness for your child, you're going to have to be part of the process.

7

Why Your Child Needs "Gym"

"The right education must tune the strings of the body and mind to perfect spiritual harmony."

—PLATO

IF YOU WERE OFFERED a program that enhanced your child's physical and mental health, academic performance, social development, and self-concept, would you turn it down? What if it also promoted an appreciation for life-long physical activity, and there was no additional charge above and beyond what you were already paying for your child's schooling?

Such a program exists. And, surprisingly, parents have been known to reject it—sometimes even vehemently.

It's called physical education. And the reason we don't blink an eye when budget constraints remove it from the curriculum is that for many of us the mere idea of what we called "gym" induces, at best, a cringe and, at worst, a stomach turned to knots.

Perhaps you remember the agony of waiting to be chosen by team captains. Trying to avoid the dreaded dodgeball. Being forced to climb a very long rope, in front of an "audience," when you were scared to death of heights—and rope burns. How about being made to jump the "horse" without any instruction at all? Did you pray the teacher would look the other way so you could run around it, raise your arms in victory, and pretend you'd hurdled it like an Olympic gymnast?

Maybe you recall unbridled competition. You might have vivid recollections of never being skilled or strong enough. Or, worst of all, of being eliminated and made to sit against the wall and watch everyone else have fun when all you wanted was the chance to play.

Unless you were one of the athletic kids or simply thrived on competition, you remember it all painfully well. So why, as a caring parent, would you want your child to endure such torture? Why, as a taxpayer, should you finance the torture of other innocent children in town?

Even if these aren't your recollections—if you see "phys ed" as mere "fun and games"—you might wonder why you should sanction and fund time spent running around getting sweaty. After all, there's so much for children to *learn* and little enough time to do it in.

Unfortunately, school board members, superintendents, principals, and others with the power to eliminate physical education from the curriculum are wondering the same things. Regardless of which viewpoint they hold of PE—frill or fear fest—it means that, when the budget gets tight, by all means, eliminate dodgeball!

But physical education (and, yes, that is the correct name for this content area, *not* the name of the place in which it is typically held or some abbreviation that sounds like a weird kind of soft drink) is not just about dodgeball anymore. In all honesty it never should have been about dodgeball. But times change, and we learn—both from our mistakes and from everything that's new and wonderful to know, like what recent brain research is showing us about the remarkable connection between our minds and our bodies.

In this chapter we'll explore the reasons that physical education (it's OK to call it by its initials: PE) should be a part of your child's school, whether it's preschool or elementary school. We'll look at why your child needs and deserves a quality physical education program. We'll define what *quality* means in terms of physical education, contrasting it with what we now know to be "bad" PE. We'll also review the current state of physical education throughout the United States and determine what you, as a caring parent, can do to improve it.

Why PE?

Given the staggering rates of childhood and adult obesity and the health risk factors appearing at younger and younger ages, it would seem the answer

The Dodgeball Debate

Some people like dodgeball. They have fond memories of the adrenaline rush and can't imagine why a number of schools are banning it. After all, doesn't it teach throwing, catching, and dodging skills? And don't the kids enjoy it?

Unfortunately, some of the adults who enjoyed it as children—and still do—are today's physical education teachers. And they enjoyed it because they were among the skilled players. They were athletic and quick and had a killer aim.

But in a university class composed of both physical education majors and future classroom teachers, the other half of the story is told when the game is played or discussed. The future classroom teachers weren't necessarily among the athletically gifted. They remember hearts pounding—not with excitement but in terror of being walloped or of looking stupid. They remember the viciousness of some of the throws and the glee in the eyes of the kids who hit their intended targets. They remember being eliminated first—or *trying* to be—and sitting on the sidelines, feeling left out.

Whether you're on the side that believes the game teaches important movement skills or teaches kids it's a tough world out there or on the side that feels it's physically and emotionally harmful, potentially even promoting aggression and bullying, you have to admit that exercise can be tough enough without children being taught it's downright painful. You have to admit the game offers little physical activity or skill development to those eliminated—or maybe to those who aren't!

As Mary Marks, health and PE coordinator for the Fairfax County Public Schools in Fairfax, Virginia, points out, we wouldn't teach academic subjects by eliminating children. Imagine trying to teach kids to read by eliminating the slowest—having them stumble over a word and forcing them to put down their books and sit on the sidelines. If that seems preposterous to you, then so should the idea of teaching motor skills through elimination games.

NASPE has named dodgeball an inappropriate activity, and it has the backing of a number of physical education experts who see no value—educational, social, or otherwise—in the game. And though they may have enjoyed it as kids—and the kids who still like it may well choose to play it at recess—teachers of the new PE also recognize it has no place in their programs.

If your child is being forced to play this game and others like it, speak up. Physical education shouldn't be about pain and embarrassment. It shouldn't be a mandate to "kill or be killed." Physical education should be about how *good* physical activity can feel.

to the question posed in the heading is obvious. Especially when we consider how many of these health problems are a result of sedentary living.

Children need to get moving. And physical education classes get them moving.

But, you may argue, *how much difference can PE make to a child's health? Even if children had PE every day*—and too few children do—*can it really make an impact? And what about all the negatives mentioned in the opening section? Wouldn't those turn children off to physical activity?*

Yes, all of the negatives mentioned in the opening section can certainly contribute to a lifelong dislike of physical activity. And they have—for many, many individuals who are now adults and couch potatoes. Any informal survey of a roomful of adults will confirm this.

But these adults suffered through the "old" PE, which often included endless calisthenics, fitness testing after which the results were posted (or, worse, announced), forced laps around the track (occasionally as punishment for misbehavior), "performing" in front of everyone else, and taunts from other kids and sometimes even the teacher when they failed to measure up.

This is not to say that developmentally inappropriate physical education programs no longer exist. They do and in numbers sufficient enough to cause real concern. But things are definitely changing for the better (a topic we'll explore more fully later in the chapter). And the evidence shows that today's quality physical education classes do make an impact because they *encourage* lifelong physical activity by providing children with the information, skills, and attitude they need to be physically active for a lifetime.

Where else are kids going to get all that? Physical education specialists are trained to know the benefits of physical activity and to impart that information to their students. But as Judy Young, executive director of the National Association for Sport and Physical Education (NASPE), says, it's not enough just to know physical activity promotes good health. Children need to know *how* and to be motivated and confident enough to go for it. PE teachers can offer that as well. Additionally, they can help children understand that superior athletic skill isn't required to lead an active lifestyle. Nor is it necessary to become an exercise "fanatic" to be fit.

For many children physical education class is their only opportunity to learn about the relationships among exercise, nutrition, and health. It's their only opportunity to acquire and refine motor skills. For some it's their only opportunity to move vigorously on a regular basis! Other physical activity programs depend on such factors as affordability, making the cut, parent support, and transportation.

According to the Task Force on Community Preventive Services (operated under the auspices of the Centers for Disease Control and Prevention), school-based PE classes are effective in improving both physical activity levels and physical fitness in students. The task force reviewed fourteen published studies, all of which determined children participating in PE show increases in physical fitness. The Centers for Disease Control (CDC) and the U.S. surgeon general concur. A scientific report published by the CDC showed a strong indication that PE programs in schools result in greater physical activity. And the surgeon general's report calls school-based physical education "the most widely available resource for promoting physical activity among young people in the United States."

One study, in fact, showed that teenagers taking PE every day were twice as likely to exercise outside of school! Even if they didn't get PE daily, they were still 44 percent more likely to get out and move than those teens who didn't take physical education.

Of course that only makes sense. We know for ourselves we're more likely to have the energy and motivation to keep moving once we've started. (Wasn't that Newton's first law? An object in motion remains in motion.) On the other hand, once we've plunked ourselves down on the couch for any length of time, there's little to no energy or motivation to get back up! If that's the case in the short term, it doesn't take much imagination to see how the problem is exacerbated over the long haul—how living life from a sitting position can become the norm.

As a result of recent research and the frightening statistics concerning children's health, the Task Force on Community Preventive Services, the CDC, the surgeon general, and others—including the American Heart Association, the American Academy of Pediatrics, Healthy People 2010, and a report developed at former president Clinton's request, entitled "Promoting Health for Young People Through Physical Activity and Sports"—all recommend that children, from pre-kindergarten to grade twelve, participate in quality physical education classes on a daily basis.

Even Congress has gotten into the act, determining that, among other things:

- Physical education is essential to the development of growing children.
- Physical education helps improve the overall health of children by improving their cardiovascular endurance, muscular strength and power, and flexibility and by enhancing weight regulation, bone development, posture, skillful moving, active lifestyle habits, and constructive use of leisure time.
- Physical education helps improve self-esteem, interpersonal relationships, responsible behavior, and independence of children.
- Children who participate in high-quality physical education programs tend to be healthier and more physically fit.

Consequently, in 2000, Congress approved a spending bill that included a $5 million appropriation for the Physical Education for Progress (PEP) Act—the funds to be used to "initiate, expand, and improve physical education programs for all K–12 students." In 2001 they increased the appropriation to $50 million. And by the time this book is in your hands, it's expected to be at $70 million!

However, despite support from these many groups, there's still one final argument made by PE's opponents. As Alma Allen, one of two school board members who voted against Texas's reinstatement of required PE, commented: "If you have [mandatory] PE, you can have kids that are healthy but dumb—and that's not what we want." Other dissenters agree, insisting that the purpose of schools is the promotion of academics, not physical fitness.

The prevailing belief? The body has nothing to do with the mind. And, by the way, that the latter is far superior to the former.

What utter nonsense! As we learned in Chapter 3, there is no dichotomy between mind and body. Quite the opposite, as science continues to show. When we disengage the body from the mind, the latter suffers. When we acknowledge that people are thinking, feeling, *moving* human beings, all three domains benefit.

Even Plato, a man best known for the workings of his mind, realized the folly of neglecting one at the expense of the other. He was convinced that physical activity stimulated intellectual development—long before brain scans, electrodes, and other such high-tech tools were available to prove him right.

And they have indeed proved him right. Among other things, the research shows that physically active students are more likely to be alert, academically motivated, *and* successful. There are also studies demonstrating that children learn better when they're actively engaged and that students taking daily PE perform better academically than those who don't take PE.

John J. Ratey, clinical associate professor of psychiatry at Harvard Medical School, considers it a "crime" that physical education is being cut from schools when we have so much research showing it benefits children academically as well as physically. Speaking at a recent conference entitled "Learning and the Brain," Ratey shared research concluding that exercise boosts brain power by increasing blood flow and stimulating cell growth. It helps, he said, to consider the brain a muscle. After all, everybody knows exercise benefits muscles.

So physical education's dissenters needn't worry about students having brawn but no brain. Science shows that's not likely to happen.

Why PE for Preschoolers?

If your child is not yet in the primary grades, you might feel the preceding information is for future reference only. But actually that's not so. If your child is enrolled in a preschool or child-care program, it's definitely to her benefit that the program include physical education among its offerings.

The Council on Physical Education for Children (COPEC, a council within NASPE), the National Association for the Education of Young Children (NAEYC), and the U.S. Department of Health and Human Services all recommend that physical education be offered to children enrolled in preschool programs. There are a number of reasons why.

First, habits are formed early in life. We don't wait until our children are in elementary school to teach them to brush their teeth, bathe, or eat the right foods. So why should children wait until they're school-aged to learn about physical activity? To begin acquiring the skills they need to successfully participate in it and to understand why it matters? There's evidence to show that even among children as young as three and four, those who are less active tend to stay less active later in childhood than the rest of their peers. And, as we've previously discussed, individuals who are less active in childhood remain less active as adults.

Furthermore, early childhood is the best period for the acquisition of fundamental movement skills. And as we explored in Chapter 5, motor skills don't take care of themselves. Not even basic body management skills—body-part identification, spatial awareness, and such abilities as stopping on signal—take care of themselves to the extent that we'd want for our children. Many a child has arrived in the early and even upper-elementary grades not knowing his elbows from his shoulders, unable to line up without getting too close to someone else, or lacking the ability to come to a timely halt when faced with an unexpected (or even an expected!) obstacle. And many a child has failed to develop mature patterns for basic motor skills.

These are the children who eventually lose confidence in their ability to play like the other kids. They feel clumsy and inferior and, to avoid humiliation, avoid physical activity. They grow up with the belief that they "can't throw," "can't dance," are "uncoordinated," or are "lousy at anything physical." They become the couch potatoes among us.

Someone needs to teach children where their elbows and shoulders are, about the space immediately surrounding their bodies (and what it's possible to do within it), how to stop and start, and the many ways in which it's possible to move. Someone needs to offer instruction, practice opportunities, assessment, and the chance to fine-tune. And that someone should have a plan.

Too often, even when early childhood professionals fully believe in the value of movement for young children and, with no false intent, assure parents that movement is very much a part of the program, what they mean is that they let the children go out to play once or twice a day. Maybe they put on a CD during "circle time" and encourage the children to dance for a few minutes. Or they might set up an obstacle course once a week and give the children some time to explore it.

These professionals honestly believe they're meeting the children's movement needs—because, unless movement or early childhood physical education was part of their pre- or in-service training, they just don't know any better. (Unfortunately, it's often the case that movement education is shortchanged in early childhood training.)

But these scenarios don't begin to meet children's fitness and motor development needs. Even if the children were doing all of the above, these scenarios couldn't be considered physical *education*. Movement lessons need to be planned and taught just as other lessons are taught in early childhood. As Linda Carson, professor at West Virginia University and director of the West Virginia Motor Development Center, writes in the September 2001 issue of *Teaching Elementary Physical Education*:

> Many preschool children in homes, agencies, centers, and schools participate in physical activities that are "unplanned" and self-selected. While self-selected play is important for young children, so is movement instruction that has been planned, sequenced, and delivered by an informed teacher. . . . Without planned instruction and teacher-directed practice opportunities, the under-informed staff is really leaving movement learning and the acquisition and improvement of motor skills to chance.

Dr. Carson goes on to say that simply offering toys, props, and a "gross motor area" is not enough—that parents and teachers would never leave children's cognitive development to chance. She insists, "They would not advocate learning to read or communicate by having their children enter a 'gross cognitive area' where children could engage in self-selected 'reading play' with a variety of books."

She's absolutely right. The notion of leaving cognitive or, for that matter, social/emotional development to chance is completely ludicrous. (Do we thrust children out into the world and let them figure out how to get along in it on their own?) Yet we feel no similar sense of absurdity at the idea of leaving physical development to chance—that all we need to do is let the children play and they'll become ready for all the physical challenges life will bring their way.

COPEC has developed a position statement entitled "Appropriate Practices in Movement Programs for Young Children Ages 3–5." The introduction includes the following paragraph:

> Childhood is the time to begin the development of active, healthy lifestyles. The development of skills, knowledge, and attitudes leading to active, healthy lifestyles must be taught. Placing the child on the road to a lifetime of movement should begin early to ensure a lifetime of good health.

How early? Although the COPEC document pertains to preschool-aged children, as evidenced by Chapter 4, it's never too early to start thinking about your child's physical education. Regardless of whether you have a preschooler, a toddler, or an infant enrolled in an early childhood setting, you should do whatever it takes to ensure his or her physical development receives as much attention as do cognitive and social/emotional development.

What's "Good" PE?

Before we consider what comprises a quality physical education program, let's look at some of the elements of "bad" PE. They include, but are not limited to, the following:

- The curriculum is based on the teacher's interests and preferences, often including what she or he has been doing for decades.

- The curriculum consists of traditional sports or activities intended to prepare children only to play sports. Sometimes this is the case when the person responsible for PE is a coach first and an educator second.

- Competition reigns. (A PE major not long ago watched a class of second-graders playing kickball. As one little boy rounded third base and headed for home, the *teacher* threw the ball that got him out. In fact he threw the ball so hard he knocked the child down and caused him to cry. The lesson those second-graders learned that day was that you do whatever it takes to win. A second message may have been that, no matter how hard you try, someone bigger and more powerful is going to come along and keep you from getting to "home plate.")

- Activities are geared only toward the athletically gifted. Students who can't keep up or are forced to try activities beyond their capabilities fall further and further behind.

- The teacher uses physical activity, like running the track or doing push-ups, as punishment for bad behavior in class. (Does this give the impression that physical activity is supposed to be something that makes us feel good? Physical activity should be something we do to *reward* ourselves.)

- The teacher groups students by choosing team captains, who then pick their teams. Not only is this humiliating for students consistently chosen last, but also it uses time that could be better spent in activity.

- Free play is considered physical education time.

- Military-style exercises are the order of the day.

- Elimination games rule. These kinds of activities tend to eliminate the children who most need to move and practice.

- More time is spent in sedentary activity, like taking attendance, than in moving. (Researchers who watched two fifth-grade classes in Texas discovered that, in forty-minute sessions, fewer than four minutes were spent in moderate to vigorous activity.)

In general, a good physical education program prepares children for a lifetime of physical activity by teaching movement skills and elements and health-related fitness principles. But it can do this only if all the children are involved almost all the time. That requires:

- **A reasonable student-to-teacher ratio.** Many physical education teachers are faced with more than thirty children at a time.

- **A facility that allows children to take part regardless of weather or other school functions.** The gym should not be "borrowed" for a school assembly or book fair, nor should physical education take place in the cafeteria or other area where students have to "work around" the environment.

- **Enough equipment for everyone.** Children shouldn't have to spend what little time they have in PE waiting to use a ball or a hoop.

- **Teaching methods and activities that allow for individual differences in skill level.** Generally a direct, "command-style" approach that requires all children to do the same thing at the same time fails in this regard. Problem-solving methods allowing for a variety of responses to a single challenge (for example: "Find three ways to move in a forward direction across the balance beam") are more developmentally appropriate for young children.

The National Association for Sport and Physical Education, as you might expect, is even more specific concerning what qualifies as quality in PE. It has devised the following checklist for principals, teachers, and parents that allows for an evaluation of their school's PE program.

1. Is physical education taught by a qualified teacher with a degree in physical education?
2. Do students receive formal instruction in physical education for a minimum of 150 minutes per week (for elementary-school students) and 225 minutes per week (middle- and high-school students)?
3. Is the physical education class size (25–30) consistent with safe, effective instruction?
4. Are there adequate funds to provide enough equipment for every student to participate?
5. Is technology incorporated on a regular and continuing basis?
6. Are indoor and outdoor facilities adequate and sufficient?
7. Is there a written, sequential curriculum based on the national and/or state physical education content standards?

8. Is assessment an integral part of the physical education program, and is it aligned with the state and/or national content standards?
9. Does the program provide for maximum participation and successful learning for every student?
10. Does the program address development of the whole student, including the physical, cognitive, and affective domains?

Perhaps you've gotten wind of something called the "new PE." It's a philosophy of physical education becoming more prominent throughout the United States—and, as much as possible, it meets the preceding criteria. The focus, rather than being on competitive sports and the athletically gifted, is on making physical activity feel good for everyone. Students engage in many cooperative activities. They get to try lots of different things, ensuring they'll find something they particularly enjoy. They learn what it takes to become a physically fit person.

In the new PE, everyone has the chance to participate. Because there's opportunity for success at all levels of skill development, no child has to master the arts of bench warming or hiding in the background. Testing is less important than inspiring children to be physically active. Students aren't mortified by the selection of teams, as that process is more likely based on eye color, birth dates, or whether one has a brother or a sister.

And the new PE is about recognizing and educating the whole child. As mentioned, the three domains of child development don't evolve in isolation from one another. A quality physical education program that teaches children to move well will bolster self-confidence, while also helping children discover the value of rules and the joys of working and playing together—all of which fall under social/emotional development. At the same time, children will physically experience concepts—like high and low, wide and narrow, slow and fast, cause and effect—that have implications for the cognitive domain.

This integrative approach is especially important during the early childhood years, when so much is at stake in a child's development—when educating the whole child is essential to her reaching her full potential.

This is some of what the new PE—quality PE—is all about. This is the physical education your child deserves.

The PE Hall of Shame

In 1992, Neil Williams, chairman of the Health and Physical Education Department at Eastern Connecticut State University, wrote his first article listing childhood games he deemed inappropriate for physical education classes. The article appeared in the *Journal of Physical Education, Recreation & Dance*. Since then he has twice updated the list.

Following are the games that, because they eliminate, intimidate, or make children wait, are currently included in Dr. Williams's "Physical Education Hall of Shame":

- Dodgeball
- Duck, Duck, Goose
- Messy Backyard
- Kickball
- Musical Chairs
- Relay Races
- Steal the Bacon
- Line Soccer
- Red Rover
- Simon Says
- Spud
- Tag

Good PE for the Pre-K Set

The National Association for the Education of Young Children considers "early childhood" to be birth to age eight. Since these are the years covered in this book, it would seem any mention of early childhood physical education would therefore encompass children birth to eight. But there are some qualifications that need to be made here. Just because children comprising this eight-year span all fall under one heading (early childhood), that doesn't mean there aren't significant differences among them. And those differences require special care to be taken.

Naturally, physical education for infants (see Chapter 4) doesn't have the same meaning as does PE for older children. And, although children in the primary grades have more in common developmentally with preschoolers than with their upper-elementary counterparts, their movement, cognitive, and social/emotional capabilities are more advanced than those of toddlers and preschoolers. That means the possibilities for their PE program are considerably greater.

Unfortunately, if your preschooler is already attending public school and receiving physical education, he may well be receiving it from someone who's aware of this at only the most rudimentary level because the teacher had no—or little—training in early childhood studies (because public pre-school is a fairly new trend). When PE teachers are trained primarily in athletics, they're often at a loss when faced with the reality of teaching four- and five-year-olds. They may see them as smaller versions of primary-grade children and simply "water down" the elementary curriculum. But the differences go well beyond size, as anyone who's studied child development knows.

On the other hand, if your preschooler (or toddler) is in a private preschool or child-care setting, her "PE teacher" may well be someone without a background in either child or motor development. Often it's someone who enjoys the company of children and comes once a week, with fun equipment and props, to play with the kids. The children have a great time and certainly learn some things along the way, including enjoyment of physical activity. But unless there's a well-informed, sequential plan, any motor skill development may be accidental.

In the best of all worlds, pre-K children (as well as their older peers) receive movement instruction from someone who knows both child development and developmentally appropriate physical education. This instructor would therefore know that, for preschoolers and toddlers:

- The initial emphasis in a PE program should be on basics such as body and spatial awareness. As simplistic as it may sound, children must be able to identify body parts before they can use them. They must understand the concept of personal space before they can move successfully among others. The PE teacher will then be able to concentrate on the most fundamental locomotor and nonlocomotor skills, explored in a developmental progression, and the variety of ways in which it's possible to perform them (using the movement elements described in Chapter 5).

- Competition and elimination have no place in the movement program, and fun is absolutely of the essence.

- Repetition—lots of it—is a must if the children are to experience success and improve their skills.

- Waiting around is even less appropriate than it is for primary-grade children. Not only does it take time that's better spent moving, young children are not very good at it.

- A smaller student-teacher ratio is needed than for elementary-aged children. The most learning will take place when the ratio is no higher than ten to one.

Many physical education teachers who've previously worked only with children in kindergarten and up are amazed to discover just how different the pre-K set is. They often comment it's as though preschoolers are a "whole different animal" (and toddlers still another). In essence it's true. There are enough distinctions between toddlers and preschoolers and between preschoolers and elementary-aged children to require different approaches to the teaching of physical education. Anyone responsible for teaching PE to the pre-K set should be aware of that first and foremost.

The Current State of PE

Here's the situation as it now stands. Despite the calls of Congress, Healthy People 2000 and 2010, the Centers for Disease Control, the American Academy of Pediatrics, the National Association of State Boards of Education, and others to offer children daily physical education, only 78 percent of states in the United States require elementary schools to teach PE at all. And 40 percent of those allow students to be exempted from PE for at least one grading period if they, among other reasons:

- Have a cognitive disability
- Participate in community sports activities

- Participate in other school activities
- Have a permanent physical disability
- Have religious beliefs prohibiting them from participation

In some instances a kid can get out of PE if his parents send a note attesting that the child works out at a gym. It makes you wonder: should students similarly be exempted from English classes because they speak the language outside of school?

And daily PE? Only one state—Illinois—mandates physical education every day for all students. But school districts within the state have the option of requesting a waiver from the mandate. In February 2002 the Chicago public school system reapplied for its PE waiver for elementary schools, preferring to offer it only twice a week. And among the activities the state allows as substitutions for physical education are recess and band!

On the other hand (putting a positive spin on things) 8 percent of elementary schools do provide daily physical education, despite the fact that it's not required. And there are only two states—Colorado and South Dakota—that have no legislative mandate for PE at all. But since it's left to the individual school districts to decide what to do about it, that doesn't mean there's no physical education in Colorado and South Dakota.

Unfortunately, only 39.7 percent of elementary schools in this country require physical education for kindergarten, which seems to indicate a mindset that PE is only preparation for sports participation. While it's certainly true kindergartners are not ready for that kind of physical education (it shouldn't be offered to any students), it's also true that kindergartners may need quality PE even more than their older counterparts. After all, they're still very much in the process of developing their movement skills and forming lifelong habits. And if they've had no formal physical education prior to kindergarten, they shouldn't have to wait until first grade to get it!

As far as teacher certification is concerned, only four states (Delaware, Illinois, Michigan, and Missouri) allow only certified specialists to teach PE. (Just over 50 percent of the states and 70 percent of the school districts require their newly hired PE teachers to have an undergraduate or graduate degree in physical education or a related field.) Forty-five states recommend specialists for PE but do allow classroom teachers, who've often had no training in the discipline, to teach it. In California, for example, elementary-school students are supposed to get two hundred minutes of physical education every ten days. But because classroom teachers are so often responsible for PE, "physical education" can turn into either recess or a study period.

You have to wonder why it's OK for noncertified instructors or teachers with no training or degree in the discipline to teach physical education. Do schools hire noncertified instructors to teach science or math? Would they hire someone with no experience speaking foreign languages to conduct Spanish classes? Why is an exception made for physical education, a subject that requires, among other things, knowledge of kinesiology (the study of human movement), physiology (the study of living organisms), and pedagogy (the study of teaching)? Is there a widespread belief that if a person has a body, he's automatically equipped with the knowledge of how to use it?

Then there's the issue of physical activity used as punishment. Only 2 percent of the states and 15.2 percent of school districts prohibit schools from using physical activity as punishment for bad behavior in the gym. Approximately 28 percent of the states and 43.8 percent of the districts actively discourage the practice.

NASPE's executive director, Judy Young, says physical education in this country is still "a work in progress," requiring more time, resources, and attention to meeting standards. She gives PE in the United States an overall grade of C. But there are signs of progress. In 1995 physical education requirements were phased out of Texas public schools to allow more time for academics. However, with recent awareness of the crisis in children's health and fitness came the decision in 2002 to reinstate mandatory PE. Elementary school students will now be required to take a minimum of 135 minutes of physical education a week.

We still have a long way to go, of course. The trend, over the last twenty years, has been a steady decline in time spent in physical education. That trend must now be reversed. More states must come to the realization that Texas did: children have both minds *and* bodies requiring our attention.

The goal, according to NASPE and the National Association of State Boards of Education, is daily PE—the equivalent of at least 150 minutes a week—for all elementary-school students. And it has to be quality PE, taught by certified teachers trained in physical education.

What's a Parent to Do?

In 2000, Tommy Thompson, chairperson of the Health, Physical Education, and Recreation Department at the University of North Carolina at Pembroke, wrote an article called "PE and the 'Normal' American Child." In it he declared parents to be "a main adversary" of physical education in America.

The reason? Thompson contends parents (and educational administrators) consider it "normal" for a child to watch TV four to five hours a day, sit at a computer for another three to four hours, be chauffeured everywhere, eat a lot of junk food, and shun movement in general and physical education in particular. In short Thompson states: "Many parents seem to believe that it is only to be expected that their children will sit a lot and eat a lot." It is then left to physical educators to "try to get unfit, overweight, unmotivated, and generally lazy children to move and be active."

Though his words are harsh, Thompson lays the blame on lack of information about the importance of physical activity and its connection to intellectual development. This book has provided you with a good deal of information about both of these topics. And you certainly wouldn't be reading it if you weren't already interested in the role of physical activity in your child's life. It's therefore up to you and others like you to lead the charge to change what's considered normal behavior for today's children and to ensure quality physical education is part of that change.

The most important thing you can do, where the latter is concerned, is to become an advocate. Regardless of your own personal experiences with it, you have to put the past in the past and look toward the future, for your child's sake.

Perhaps it's even better if your experiences with PE were horrendous—if the memory of it sends shivers down your spine. Since you have personal knowledge of "bad" PE, you're better equipped and certainly more motivated to fight for quality PE for your son or daughter.

As a parent and a taxpayer you are the school's "customer." And, as we know, the customer is always right. There are surveys, conducted by both the American Obesity Association and NASPE, showing that parents do strongly oppose cutbacks in PE. Eighty percent of parents questioned said they didn't want PE classes cut in favor of more academic time. Yet PE programs continue to be cut. The reason these "customers" are being ignored? Perhaps they, although in the vast majority, have failed to make themselves heard. That has to change. As the saying goes, the squeaky wheel gets the grease. So start squeaking!

Download NASPE's "Physical Education Checkup" at aahperd.org /naspe, and begin asking questions. Delve even deeper than the questionnaire does, finding out:

- What the children are doing in class. Are they only playing games? Are children being eliminated?

- What teaching methods are being employed. Are all of the children expected to do the same thing at the same time, regardless of skill level? Is the teacher focusing on the most skilled? Or is he teaching "to the middle," resulting in frustration for the less physically skilled and boredom for the talented students?

- How much time is spent *moving*. Are the children waiting turns, lining up, or standing around listening to endless instructions?

- Whether or not students are allowed to substitute something else for PE.

If you're not satisfied with the answers, talk with your principal. A number of PE teachers say their greatest obstacle is lack of administrative support. But the reason for the lack of support may well be lack of knowledge on the principal's part. It's quite possible the principal also experienced the "gym class from hell" as a child and is unaware of the changes that have occurred in the field. Keeping up with advances in every discipline is a tremendous challenge.

In a 2001 article in *Principal,* Terry Beasley wrote of the "physical education" program he inherited when he became principal of an elementary school in Alabama. There were two instructors for the 360 second- and third-graders, one of whom could usually be found in his truck, reading a newspaper, and the other of whom sat at a picnic table reading romance novels. The "curriculum," which never varied, consisted of games on Monday, jogging on Tuesday and Thursday, and free play on Wednesday and Friday. The instructors also used inappropriate language, and children were frequently injured.

It's hard to imagine a worse program. It's hard to imagine the school's former principal allowed it to exist, let alone continue. But she or he may not have known any better. Or she or he had so many other things with which to be concerned that, without a good reason to make a change (parents speaking up), it was easier to retain the status quo.

Don't settle for the status quo for your child. If you get no satisfaction from your principal, there's always the school board, the state department of education, and even legislators. Involve your neighbors and the PTA, using the information in this chapter and Chapter 3 to help them understand the importance of physical activity and the connection between mind and body. Call on local medical professionals to lend support.

There are plenty of organizations offering support, too. NASPE has a number of materials available to help you advocate for physical education. Some are available for a small fee; others are free with a self-addressed, stamped envelope. Check out their website (aahperd.org/naspe) or call them at 800-213-7193, extension 410.

At the CDC website (cdc.gov), you can find the surgeon general's report "Physical Activity and Health," or you can download "Promote Lifelong Physical Activity Among Young People," a report summarizing the benefits of physical activity, as well as actions parents, administrators, and school board members can take.

And at the P.E.4Life website (pe4life.org), you can learn about the community action kit produced in association with NASPE and publisher Human Kinetics. The kit is available to consumers for just a $5.50 shipping charge and includes both a video and a CD-ROM to help you advocate for physical education in your area. The video gives you a great look at the new

PE and provides reasons that physical activity and physical education are important for children. The CD-ROM provides you with PowerPoint presentations, supporting handouts, sample letters of invitation, and links to helpful websites so you can go into battle fully prepared.

Of course you'll have to be patient as you wage your battle. As you know, change doesn't happen overnight. And the changes you generate may be smaller than what you'd hoped for. For example, you may not be able to have specialists teaching physical education at your child's school. But you might successfully lobby for the classroom teachers to attend workshops related to physical education. (For instance, in California, where classroom teachers often teach PE, California Polytechnic State University in San Luis Obispo sponsors a conference every summer at which physical education experts present workshops.) Or you might be able to get the school to hire a physical education consultant to write a curriculum the classroom teachers can use.

If your child is still among the pre-K set, don't wait to begin waging your battle. First, if he's not yet enrolled in a preschool or child-care setting, you can choose one that offers movement education conducted by someone who knows both children and movement. When you interview centers, let them know movement is important to you.

If your child is already enrolled in a center, speak up if there's no movement program. If the director indicates (as many have and continue to do) they don't have time for movement because they're too busy "preparing children for elementary-school academics" (yes, the pressure for accountability has even reached this level), tell her you don't believe it's possible to have one without the other. Bring her this book, *Smart Moves* (see Resources), or any other literature citing the connection between brain and body.

If funding for a qualified instructor is a problem, let the director know you'd be willing to pay a few extra dollars a week to make physical education possible. If it's not possible to bring in a movement specialist, perhaps there's a program available locally, like the motor development lab at West Virginia University, that the children can attend at least once a week.

And begin checking out your local elementary school's PE program—or lack thereof—now. It's never too soon to think about your child's physical education, and it's never too soon to become an advocate.

8

Reading, Writing, 'Rithmetic— and Recess!

"Man does not cease to play because he grows old. Man grows old because he ceases to play."

—George Bernard Shaw

Mother Nature gave us everything we need to develop to our full potential. But when we do things like confining infants for long periods of time or placing young children in situations for which they're simply not ready, we do a great job of ignoring her. Similarly, when we insist on removing recess—or outdoor time—from the school day and children's lives, we ignore what we know about who children are and how they learn and grow.

What is this arrogance that makes us believe we can do better than what nature intended—that we can improve on nature's design? Are we so obsessed with what we perceive as "achievement" that we're willing to have our children give up everything else, including joy, imagination, connection with nature, and even physical fitness, to attain it?

Apparently so. Because despite what we know to be true about children—that is, what the *research* shows—recess (child-initiated, unstructured play during the school day) is going the way of the dinosaurs in states all over the country. According to some estimates, 40 percent of schools have already eliminated recess or are considering the idea. Some cities, like

Atlanta, have abolished recess completely and are building new elementary schools without playgrounds.

The reason, of course, is today's pervasive emphasis on academics, accountability, and standardized testing. Politicians, administrators, and, yes, even parents seem to have decided that memorizing facts and passing tests are the only valid forms of learning worthy of our children's time. They've forgotten—if they ever truly knew—that rote memorization and studying to pass a test are not actually learning at all.

The irony, however, is that the research shows children learn better when given breaks. So educational policies that keep children at their desks for extended periods to maximize time spent on academics are not based on scientific findings. In fact these policies are *contrary* to scientific data. Which means we may not only be asking our children to give up such "luxuries" as joy and imagination; we may also be jeopardizing the very goal we wish to reach: our children's success in school and life.

This chapter explores the value of recess. Yes, we will look at it in terms of its benefits to our children's education. But we'll also look well beyond the academic—to the education offered through play and by exposure to nature and the outdoors. We'll consider the role of recess in stimulating the imagination and why that's so important to both our children and the future of our society. And, of course, we'll delve into what you, as a parent, can do to ensure your child has the same opportunities and the same right to play that you had.

But, first, having spent an entire chapter on the importance of physical education in the schools, let's look at how recess differs from physical education and why they're both necessary.

Why Recess Is Different from PE

If the development of motor skills and physical fitness were the only benefits of recess, then schools offering a daily, developmentally appropriate physical education class might feel justified in eliminating recess from their programs. But there are two major points to be considered here: First, as mentioned in the last chapter, daily physical education is about as rare as purple dinosaurs. Second, recess has much more to offer than the development of motor skills and physical fitness. It's true that recess certainly contributes to these outcomes; it is in the outdoors that children can fully and freely experience large motor skills like running, leaping, and jumping, manipulative skills such as throwing, catching, and striking, and gymnastics skills like climbing and balancing. But, because it is unstructured, recess also has a great deal more to offer young children.

Physical education is organized and planned. It is an instructional program in which children are expected to participate in specific activities and achieve certain results. In that way it is like almost every other aspect of the school day.

Recess, on the other hand, is not organized and planned. It is, in fact, a *break* from structure as well as a break from all of those expectations. As such children are allowed to engage in choice: choice of activities, choice of companions. Having already spent a good deal of time with other children, they may also choose *no* companions—to be alone, in solitary reflection. All of these options benefit children, who need to learn to socialize, to contemplate, and to make choices. The latter is absolutely essential to personal responsibility and to problem-solving skills; all are essential to a full and rewarding life.

For many children, especially those who are hyperactive or potentially so, recess is an opportunity to blow off steam. Outdoors, children can engage in behaviors (loud, messy, and boisterous) considered unacceptable and annoying indoors. And research has shown that children are more active at recess than while outside at home.

Research also shows that prolonged confinement in classrooms results in restlessness and fidgeting. Could it be that we would have fewer children considered hyperactive if we simply allowed them an occasional break? And isn't it sad, not to mention exceedingly counterproductive, that the "problem" children are the ones who are most likely to have recess revoked due to their "misbehavior"?

Is there an adult alive who would voluntarily give up her or his daily breaks to remain hunched over work for long, uninterrupted hours at a time? Who doesn't need to occasionally stand and stretch, walk around, have a little conversation about something other than work, or, at the very least, clear the head with a brief game of computer solitaire? Even the most dedicated professional requires an occasional change of pace.

If we can't imagine hours of uninterrupted work as adults, how can we expect children, who have even less ability to stay still or to set aside their needs, to simply zip their lips and remain seated all day?

And speaking of zipping lips, recess may be the *only* time during the day when children have an opportunity to experience socialization and real communication. Neighborhoods are not what they used to be, so once the school day ends, there may be little chance for social interaction. Even if a child is involved in after-school programs with other children, the structure and organization of the program are unlikely to offer much in the way of socialization or choice.

And, of course, while in school children are generally not allowed to interact at all during class, while lining up, or when moving from one area of the school to another. Amazingly enough, in many elementary schools, children are not even allowed to talk with one another during lunch. Teachers, hovering like prison guards, are there to ensure the students spend this "free" time doing nothing but eating. One can only wonder how these children can ever be expected to live and work together in harmony as adults. When and where will they have learned how?

Finally, unlike during physical education class, recess is a time when children can simply and freely *play*. Unfortunately, much of how we feel about recess is connected to today's attitude toward play in general—that it's a waste of time that could be spent more "productively." (Many early childhood professionals fear play has become a "four-letter word.") But, regardless of how we presently feel about it, play has always been and always will be necessary for children. In fact, according to Playing for Keeps, a national nonprofit organization, play is "the single most important activity for the healthy development of young children."

The Value of Play

Isn't it ironic that a country whose constitution allows for the pursuit of happiness now feels a collective guilt about the very idea of anything fun? How did this happen? When did we begin placing so much priority on produc-

What About Bullying?

Besides lack of time, the reason most often given by school administrators for revoking recess is that there's too much bullying/bad behavior taking place on the playground during recess. Well, that may be so. But is eliminating recess the solution to the problem? If we were to follow the same logic, we would likewise eliminate math or language arts if the students were failing in *those* topics.

Chances are, a bully is a bully is a bully. And somewhere, somehow, the behavior is going to show itself. We're not eradicating the problem by eradicating recess. On the other hand, if we do see a pattern of bullying on the playground, we're alerted to the fact that there's a child in need of help.

Besides, there *are* alternatives. They may take more time and effort than simply whisking the problem under the rug, but time and effort are part and parcel of educating children. Following are some ideas:

Have more adults on the playground. In Omaha this was accomplished when Lauren Kincaid's efforts drew the attention of other parents, who volunteered to help out with recess.

Provide training in conflict resolution. When children are unable to resolve conflicts on their own, teachers, paraprofessionals, and parent volunteers should know how and when to intervene.

Provide "playground" training. IPA/USA offers tips for a safe and friendly environment on its website and also provides training for "playground teacher specialists" in the schools. Physical education teachers can do likewise. When children and adults know how to use the space and equipment—and have been taught plenty of games to play—there are likely to be fewer problems during recess.

Offer recess before lunch. Chip Wood, in his book *Time to Teach, Time to Learn: Changing the Pace of School*, recommends restructuring the middle of the day so that recess *precedes* lunch. Wood has found that when children are allowed to first work up an appetite, eat lunch, and then have some quiet time, the children are "more productive and engaged in the afternoon."

tivity and so little on leisure or on having a good time? Even given the Puritan work ethic, life in America has become so unbalanced that one side of the seesaw is pretty much grounded.

But why must we insist that our children, who by their very nature are playful, share these particular values? Why are we so eager for our children to "act like adults"?

As covered previously, in today's society we've come to treasure results, even in children's play. As such, home runs, goals, and points have greater worth than something that, by definition, is child-directed, open-ended, and intrinsically motivated. What results—what "product"—can we possibly expect from play, which focuses primarily on *process*? For one thing, many experts believe the adult personality is built on the child's play. According to the organization Playing for Keeps, all the skills children need to develop into functioning, productive adults originate from play. These skills include literacy, mathematical reasoning, creativity, and social skills. Among the social skills learned, the experts tell us, are the ability to share, cooperate, negotiate, compromise, make and revise rules, and take the perspective of others.

Surely we can see the value in such benefits—that these abilities will serve our children well—now and in the future. But if that's not enough benefit derived, Joan Isenberg and Mary Renck Jalongo, authors of *Creative Expression and Play in the Early Childhood Curriculum*, argue that play also:

- Enables children to explore their world
- Develops cultural understandings
- Helps children express their thoughts and feelings
- Provides opportunities to meet and solve problems

Additionally, play enables children to deal with stress and to cope with fears they can't yet understand or express. Today's young children are exposed to so much so early and must cope with much more stress than their predecessors ever did. Play gives them a necessary emotional release and helps them make sense of everything they're experiencing. And as Playing for Keeps points out, when young children act out emotion-laden scenes in their play, such as reassuring a doll that Mommy will return, they learn to cope with fears and gain the self-control that will take them to the next stage of development.

Recess: A Cultural and Historical Perspective

In Taiwan children not only have many recess periods each day but also are given five to six minutes of transition time following recess so they can settle down to their work. In Britain there are primary schools offering three daily recess periods: fifteen minutes each morning and afternoon and an hour and a half at lunch. And in Germany there's no time for play scheduled during the school day—but for most German students in both the primary and secondary grades school lasts only half a day, with children in the early primary grades going home at 10:30.

In the United States, three daily recess periods were the norm during the 1950s. Even as late as 1989, about 90 percent of the school districts in the United States had some form of recess—sometimes once and sometimes twice a day. A recent story in *U.S. News & World Report* tells us that, before the Revolutionary War, the right to play was granted even more importance than the right to bear arms. According to author Anna Mulrine, when soldiers' training interfered with the games of schoolchildren on Boston Common, the kids protested to the governor, who ordered the soldiers to withdraw. Play and recess, it seems, were considered necessary for emotional and intellectual growth.

Still, it seems recess has also long had its detractors. Writing in a publication for the National Association of Elementary School Principals, Rhonda Clements and Olga Jarrett tell us that in 1885 the superintendent of schools in Lansing, Michigan, published a report outlining eight reasons that recess should be abolished nationwide. Among the reasons were his concerns for the children's health (they rushed to the playground barely clad), safety (he worried younger children would be maimed for life by older children), and convenience (without recess children could be released earlier to help out the family at home).

Much has changed since then, of course. But have children? Has the nature of children changed so drastically since the time of the Revolutionary War? Since the 1950s? Since the 1980s? And are the children of Taiwan, Germany, and Britain all that much different from the children of the United States? If they're being granted the all-important right to play, why aren't our children?

Writing in *Education Week*, master teacher Sheila Flaxman points out that today's young children are controlled by the "expectations, whims, and rules of adults. Play is the only time they can take control of their world."

She goes on to state: "The almost daily media reports of out-of-control young people should be our warning that something is amiss in early childhood." Indeed retired psychiatrist Stuart Brown, founder of the Institute for Play in Carmel Valley, California, was quoted in *Time* magazine as saying that "play deprivation" can lead to "depression, hostility, and the loss of the things that make us human beings."

The Power of Pretend Play

When children play make-believe, they carry out plans ("I'll stand here, and then you come around the corner"), transform objects (a bunch of dandelions become vegetables on a plate), and take on roles ("I'll be the mommy, and you be the little girl"). Dorothy Singer and Jerome Singer, authors of *Make-Believe: Games and Activities for Imaginative Play*, tell us that when children play imaginative games, many benefits ensue:

> Children enlarge their vocabulary; they learn how to exercise their small and large motor skills; they learn to share, to take turns, and to cooperate. When they play with others in story-like games, children can use manners such as "please," "thank you," "excuse me." They learn how to put things in correct order and how to sequence—first we set the table, make our cookies out of clay, boil our water, and then we have the tea party. Children learn to control their impulses, and we find that they are less aggressive. Children who are imaginative players tend to smile more, laugh more, and have longer periods of attention and concentration. They become flexible and creative.

All of these benefits serve children well. But becoming more creative is no small feat.

Sadly, research has shown that creativity *peaks* in the United States at age four and a half! And school, with its insistence on conformity, academic accountability, and emphasis on competition, is largely to blame for this unnatural phenomenon.

Conversely, playfulness and creativity go hand in hand. In creativity workshops parents and teachers asked to choose words describing either creativity or play find many words common to both. They include words such as *fun*, *spontaneous*, *imaginative*, and *confidence-building*. In early childhood, creativity, like play, is also process- as opposed to product-oriented.

To be sure, we give plenty of lip service to the importance of creativity; but in the United States what we really value is the one "right" answer. And when children detect—as they do very early on—that the rewards lie with having that one right answer, they simply stop thinking creatively. And this is a far greater loss than most people realize.

Although creativity may not be easy to define (as the authors of *Creativity in Early Childhood Classrooms* point out, it's a term applied to such diverse individuals as Albert Einstein and Jim Henson), it is easy to determine why it's necessary. And not just in the arts either. We need creativity in business and industry (when Lee Iacocca turned Chrysler Corporation around, he was using creative problem solving), in science (all of our advances are the result of creativity), in education (without it there's only staleness for both student and teacher), and in life itself. Any time we solve a problem, meet a challenge, do something a bit differently from last time, we're using creativity.

Creative individuals are those who can *imagine*—who can see beyond what already exists. Thus they can imagine the solutions to problems and challenges faced. They can imagine what it's like to be someone or something else (empathy). They can imagine answers to the question "What if?" They can plan full and satisfying futures. In fact a 1999 study determined that children who play imaginatively are more often creative thinkers and effective problem solvers as they get older.

Albert Einstein, who may be as famous for his preference for "daydreaming" over academics as he is for his theory of relativity, insisted that imagination was more important than knowledge. "Knowledge is limited," he said. "Imagination encircles the world."

Today, with the ever-present, ready-made images available to our children via television, videos, and computers, the imagination may be in greater danger of extinction than at any other time in history. But it has perhaps never been more necessary.

We truly have no idea what kind of world will be awaiting our children when they grow up; things are changing so rapidly! But we can be fairly certain that problem solvers and creative thinkers will be of far greater value to society than those who excel at facts and trivia.

One thing unlikely to change is the fact that as long as there are human beings in the world there are liable to be problems in need of solving. Robert Schirrmacher, in *Art & Creative Development for Young Children*, writes: "Beyond individual development, creativity advances civilization and society by addressing and attempting to solve the global problems of hunger, poverty, disease, war, and pollution."

Can young children experience pretend play, thereby enhancing their creative potential, indoors as well as out? Absolutely. And in many developmentally appropriate preschool programs, play is still a vital part of the curriculum. But because the push for academics is now encroaching even at the preschool level, there are fewer programs than ever allowing young children to engage in the amount of play they require for healthy development. Also, once children are enrolled in the public schools, they can pretty much say good-bye to opportunities to play in the classroom despite the fact that children in kindergarten through grade three are developmentally more like preschoolers than like their upper-elementary counterparts.

As mentioned, recess ensures children have a chance to play—pretend and otherwise. And creative thinking is most likely to occur when children are provided with breaks. We have only to remember a time when a creative idea or the solution to a problem came to us while taking a walk, taking a shower, staring out the window, or drifting off to sleep (the focus for this book appeared as sleep was approaching!) to understand that a mind constantly occupied is unlikely to engage in fantasy, daydreaming, or *what-ifs*. Write the authors of *The Creative Spirit*, companion to the PBS television series: "The simplest act of physical relaxation—letting go—frees the mind to be open to new ideas."

Back to the Great Outdoors

By its very nature the outdoors is more conducive to play—more inspirational and stimulating to the imagination—than the indoors.

Think back to your own childhood. Chances are, some of your fondest memories are of outdoor activities and places. Perhaps you had a favorite climbing tree or a secret hiding place. Maybe you remember jumping rope or learning to turn cartwheels with your best friend or playing fetch with the family dog. Do you recall the smell of lilacs, the feel of the sun on the first day warm enough to take off your jacket, or the taste of a peanut butter and jelly sandwich eaten on a blanket in the park? Did you enjoy lying on your back and finding creatures in the clouds?

Now ask yourself: *Don't I want my child to have similar memories? Wonderful, happy memories?*

Unfortunately, a great many of today's children will grow up without such fond memories because today's children spend far less time outdoors than did previous generations. According to William Doherty of the University of Minnesota, over the last twenty years there has been a 25 percent decline in the time children spend playing and a 50 percent decline in time spent in unstructured outdoor activities.

As mentioned earlier in the book, television and computers provide tremendous competition for children's time and attention. Many children are home alone in the afternoons and have been instructed not to leave the house. Even when allowed outside, children are restricted to the area immediately surrounding their homes due to the perceived dangers lurking. And, as play expert Tom Jambor, from the University of Alabama at Birmingham, points out, twenty years of urbanization have slowly and methodically squeezed out children's natural play spaces, while formal play spaces, like parks and playgrounds, are often unsafe and/or unappealing. According to the National Program for Playground Safety, public playgrounds are often poorly designed, maintained, or supervised.

Recess, therefore, may be children's best—and only—opportunity to play outdoors. Without it our children will not just be missing out on memories but also on everything else the outdoors has to offer them.

To begin with, the outdoors is the best place for young children to practice and master emerging physical skills and to experience the pure joy of movement. It's also the place where they're likely to burn the most calories, which is absolutely necessary in the fight against obesity. Research has shown that children who are physically active in school are more likely to be physically active at home. (It's Newton's law of motion again.)

Also, the outside light stimulates the pineal gland, which is the part of the brain that helps regulate our biological clock, is vital to the immune system, and simply makes us feel happier. Outside light triggers the synthesis of vitamin D. And a number of studies have demonstrated that it increases academic learning and productivity.

That last point should help satisfy the needs of those who believe the physical just isn't enough—that our children *learn* something from the outdoors. But there's even more.

Young children learn much through their senses, and the outdoors is a virtual wonderland for the senses. There are different and incredible things for the children to *see* (insects, clouds, and shadows), to *hear* (traffic sounds, birdsongs, leaves rustling in the wind), to *smell* (flowers and the rain-soaked ground), to *touch* (a fuzzy caterpillar or the bark of a tree), and even to *taste* (newly fallen snow, a raindrop, or a freshly picked blueberry). Children who spend much of their time acquiring experiences through television, computers, and even books are using only two senses (hearing and sight), and this can seriously affect their perceptual abilities. Additionally, much of this learning, which falls under the content area of science, can't be acquired indoors. Nor can children who spend most of their time indoors be expected to learn to care for the environment.

Outside, children are more likely to invent games. As they do, they're able to express themselves and learn about the world in their own way. They feel safe and in control, which promotes autonomy, decision making, and organizational skills. Inventing rules for games (as preschoolers like to do) promotes an understanding of why rules are necessary. Although the children are just playing to have fun, they learn:

- Communication skills and vocabulary, as they invent, modify, and enforce rules
- Number relationships, as they keep score and count
- Social skills, as they learn to play together

All of this learning helps advance physical, social/emotional, and cognitive development—that is, the whole child.

Then, too, there's the aesthetic value of the outdoors. Because the natural world is filled with amazing sights, sounds, and textures, it's the perfect resource for the development of aesthetics in young children. Since aesthetic awareness means a heightened sensitivity to the beauty around us, it's something that can serve children well at those times when, as adolescents and adults, the world seems less than beautiful.

Finally, Mary Rivkin, author of *The Great Outdoors: Restoring Children's Right to Play Outside*, tells us there is one very basic reason that children need to experience being outside: humans evolved in the outdoors. They thus have a link with nature that can't be replaced—in fact, will be atrophied—by technology. She asks: ". . . lacking intimate association with nature, can we still be fully human?"

Children learn their values from the important adults in their lives. When we keep children indoors, they learn sedentary habits not easily changed and, more unfortunately, that the outdoor environment is of little significance.

Recess and Academics

So, we've established that recess has a lot to offer young children. But, still, you may have heard the argument that it's going to take time away from academics. And with so much for children to learn, can that really be justified? Aren't academics, on balance, more important than all that other stuff?

Well, that's debatable. But since academics *are* important, let's look at the role recess plays in helping children learn those other three Rs—and more.

Typically the early childhood and elementary curriculum consists of seven major content areas: art, language arts (comprised of listening, speaking, reading, and writing), mathematics, music, physical education, science, and social studies. Of course art, music, and physical education are too often considered expendable and are therefore either eliminated from the curriculum or given the minimum amount of time possible. That leaves what many parents and administrators consider the "essential" content areas: language arts, mathematics, science, and social studies—all of which can be experienced effectively at recess. We'll look at them one at a time.

Naturally, when children speak and listen to one another, they're using and expanding their vocabularies and learning important lessons in communication. When they move over, under, around, and through pieces of equipment, these prepositions take on meaning and relevance to them because children need to *experience* concepts to understand them fully. When children invent stories to act out, they develop skills essential to writing. These are some of the ways in which the language arts are addressed.

When children keep score, they're dealing with important mathematics concepts: counting, quantitative ideas (which number is bigger?; which score is highest?), and simple computation. When they decide on and act out a series of events, they're tackling the mathematics concept of sequencing. When they play hopscotch and jump rope, math is involved.

Throughout it all, the children are working *together*, interacting in numerous and varied ways and thereby learning valuable lessons in social studies. As children learn about themselves and about each other, they discover how they're alike and different. They explore feelings and rules for living, make decisions, and solve problems. Learned, too, is the ability to deal with conflict. In other words the children learn how to be and work together in a community.

Finally, as previously pointed out, much of the learning that takes place outside is related to science. Classroom themes typically falling into the science category include the human body and such nature-related topics as the seasons, weather, plants, and animals. Where better to experience these subjects than in the outdoors?

Consider, too, such scientific concepts as evaporation (learned when children "paint" the sidewalk or the side of the school with water), flotation (easily demonstrated with a bottle of bubbles and a wand), balance and stability (the lesson of the seesaw), gravity (why doesn't the ball stay up in the air no matter how hard we throw it?), and action and reaction (obvious during a game of tug-of-war).

Sure, we can "teach" children these concepts through the use of lectures, books, and/or demonstrations. Or we can let children really *learn* them—in such a way that the lessons remain with them for a lifetime. Young children especially learn through experience, but the research shows that, for the majority of individuals, learning by *doing* is most effective. In fact the more senses involved in the learning process, the greater the percentage of retention. As Confucius said: "What I hear, I forget. What I see, I remember. What I do, I know."

Of course we also have the issue of how recess contributes *indirectly* to the learning of academics. As mentioned, the research is quite clear on this. Even as far back as 1885 and 1901, the research showed that both children and adults learn better and more quickly when their efforts are distributed (breaks are included) than when concentrated (work is conducted in longer periods). More recently, the novelty-arousal theory has suggested that people function better when they have a change of pace. And most recently, research by experts such as Olga Jarrett, Anthony Pellegrini, and David Bjorklund has shown similar results.

According to Pellegrini and Bjorklund, because young children don't process most information as effectively as older children (due to the immaturity of their nervous systems and their lack of experience), they can especially benefit from breaks—from the practice of distributed, rather than concentrated, effort. They wonder, rightfully so, why school districts are ignoring all of this science when considering their recess policies.

With this in mind, Olga Jarrett and her colleagues approached an urban school district with a policy against recess. They received permission for two fourth-grade classes to have recess once a week so they could determine the impact on the children's behavior on recess and nonrecess days. The result was that the forty-three children became more on-task and less fidgety on days when they had recess. Sixty percent of the children, including the five suffering from attention deficit disorder, worked more and/or fidgeted less on recess days. Dr. Jarrett's research demonstrated that a fifteen-minute recess resulted in the children's being 5 percent more on-task and 9 percent less fidgety, which translated into twenty minutes saved during the day. This, of course, flies in the face of the argument that there simply isn't time for recess.

But none of this science is likely to come as a surprise to the parents of young children whose schools have eliminated recess. They don't need research findings to tell them what they can see with their own eyes: that being without recess is taking its toll on their children. Lauren Kincaid, the mother of two elementary-school children in Omaha, Nebraska, has said that, without recess, her son would come home and fall apart. He was exhausted, wound up, and angry. Surely we don't need scientific data to know that that state of mind isn't exactly conducive to learning.

What's a Parent to Do?

An online Parent Soup poll asked the question: "Do you think recess should be eliminated in elementary schools?" Fewer than 3 percent of the 1,506 parents responding said yes; more than 97 percent said no.

Parents (and, often, even teachers) are not typically consulted when decisions to abolish recess are handed down. But parents have certainly played a role in getting recess reinstated!

Rebecca Lamphere, of Virginia Beach, Virginia, wasn't even the parent of a school-age child when she began her fight. But having lived next door to an elementary school for about a year, she was troubled by the fact that she never saw children on the playground! And though she hadn't yet read the data that backed her up, she felt certain something was terribly wrong with that scenario; so she began making phone calls. What she learned from the school board administration was that recess wasn't mandatory and it was going to stay that way.

That's when Rebecca began researching the topic in earnest. She went to the library and to the computer—and then she went to the school board. It took two speeches before they decided to address the issue. Rebecca learned that of the fifty-five elementary schools in Virginia Beach, only three scheduled recess, with five others offering "walk-n-talk," an exercise of ushering children around four cones, with only moderate talking allowed! Rebecca lost the first battle when the majority of the school board voted to leave recess as it was: virtually nonexistent.

Determined not to lose the war, Rebecca started a petition and then went before the board again. She began speaking to the members one-on-one. She was told she'd need backup from professionals in the field, so she recruited the help of the director of the child development lab at a local college. Her first real victory was when Virginia Beach finally wrote a resolution stating that teachers were "allowed" to offer recess (unstructured play time). But because the resolution didn't include the word *daily*, Rebecca pushed on.

Janet Hyde-Wright, a mother in Norfolk, and Lynne Lowe, a mother in Chesapeake, joined Rebecca in the fight. Finally the state board of education heard the outcry, and in April of 2000, following two days of heated debate, they chose to write mandatory recess into the proposed standards of accreditation. But Rebecca wasn't finished. She drove to Richmond for the next three meetings, and, on July 28, 2000, it was determined that for a school in the state of Virginia to be accredited, it had to provide a daily recess for all elementary students, beginning in the fall. Virginia is now the first and only state in the country to mandate recess.

Of course not every battle waged is going to have such astonishing results. And although Lauren Kincaid (mentioned earlier in the chapter) would be thrilled to have Nebraska mandate daily recess, she's glad for the progress she's made to date in her hometown of Omaha.

There the elementary schools each set their own recess policies, at the principal's discretion. The most common practice was thirty minutes scheduled to include both lunch and recess. At some schools that entire time was spent in the cafeteria. At others, there was a fifty-fifty split. At Lauren's children's school, due to time spent lining up, the children were outside for an average of five to eight minutes.

Lauren, who was PTA president when she began her campaign, aligned with a friend, who was PTA president at another Omaha elementary school. Together they created a survey that they sent to the other PTA presidents and the elementary-school principals. What they discovered was that the parents whose children were getting the most recess daily were satisfied, whereas the parents whose children were in schools with less recess felt their children were not getting adequate physical activity. ParentsCARE (Concerned about Recess and Education) was formed.

The next step was to meet with the director of elementary education for the Omaha Public Schools. Over a period of time they provided him, teachers, and administrators with newspaper and magazine articles about children's decreasing physical fitness. Says Lauren, "When kids score low on math tests, it makes sense that math instruction gets more attention. Applying that same equation to this issue is appropriate. Societal trends are showing dramatically lower fitness levels, increasing weight, and associated health problems in children. Therefore, it follows that increased physical activity needs to be emphasized."

ParentsCARE also wrote many letters to administrators and to the newspaper. They spoke at PTA meetings, organized parents to help at recess time, got their story into the newspapers and on TV, and did whatever they could to inform teachers and paraprofessionals of the importance of recess. To date their successes include:

- Increased parent awareness of the recess practices in the elementary schools
- Increased parent participation during recess, to assist with monitoring the children, managing the equipment, and the like
- Heightened awareness of the importance of recess among the public school administrators
- Increased communication between parents and administrators
- Appointment of two ParentsCARE members to the district's elementary school–day review committee

Their two greatest wins, however, were the creation of a new recess policy and a written statement from the superintendent of schools on the importance of recess. The policy, established in February 2001, states: "Principals will be instructed to provide (aggressively pursue) a minimum of a full fifteen minutes of recess after lunch, preferably outside. Those teachers who wish to do more will be free to do so. Additionally, classroom teachers should be encouraged to give their students a second recess in the afternoon, at their (the teachers') discretion as they see the need for it in their students."

The superintendent, Dr. John Mackiel, writing in an administrative bulletin, told the story of a five-year-old in a school without recess, who had confided to a reporter that she liked to sit on the grass and look for ladybugs. Dr. Mackiel lamented the fact that childhood may have become too busy for ladybugs and encouraged the schools to include "better living through recess" in their professional development plans for the following year.

The result of all this for Lauren's children has been that their principal extended the lunch/recess period by five minutes, enabling the elementary grades to get a full fifteen minutes of recess. Is it the success Lauren had hoped for? Perhaps not. She'd love to get the thirty-five-minute lunch/

recess period increased to forty minutes, and she'd like to see an across-the-board weather policy that encourages teachers to take the children outdoors even on days when the temperature dips below twenty. But she's glad she took on the fight, no matter how difficult; and the rest of the parents in her children's school are pleased, too.

Following are some tips, compiled from the advice of Lauren, Rebecca, and others, on how you, too, can ensure your children have the right to recess.

- **Do your homework.** First, ask your child if recess is part of the school day. If so, how often does it occur? How long does it last? What happens on the playground? Find out from other parents what their children are experiencing. Then set up a meeting with your child's classroom teacher to clearly determine if, when, and how often the class has recess. Are children ever kept from recess? Why?

- **Be sensitive.** Most teachers are under tremendous pressure to achieve nearly impossible objectives. They could use a break, too!

- **Don't go it alone.** One concerned parent can be considered a rabble-rouser, but several concerned parents have influence. Recruit the parents of your children's friends and classmates. Contact the president of the school's parent or parent/teacher organization to discuss your concerns about recess. With the help of the association, set up a meeting with the school's principal.

- **Do some more homework.** If you don't like the answers you're receiving and you want to bring about change, you'll need backup in the form of research and respected professionals. Do as Lauren and Rebecca did: go to the library and to the computer and dig up as much information as you can to make your case. (You won't find any dearth of materials on either the recess or childhood obesity issue!) Contact organizations that advocate for recess and play (some of them are listed in the Resources), and build on the foundation they've already laid for you. Find a local professional who feels strongly about the need for recess and play in early childhood and recruit him or her to address school administrators and/or the school board if necessary.

- **Educate!** Make copies of the information you've accumulated, highlighting the important points, and distribute them among administrators, faculty, and other parents. Whenever possible, speak one-on-one with teachers, school board members, and parents.

- **Alert the media!** Write letters to the editors of the local newspapers, submit an opinion piece, or just call and tell them your story. Contact local radio and television stations. Invite a television feature reporter to experience recess with your children. Or, if your child's school has no recess, invite the reporter to join your child's class for a day without breaks.

- **Think big!** Work with your elected officials and school board members to ensure recess is available for every child every day in every school. Ask your PTA to include, within its state resolutions, recess as a mandatory part of each school day. Become a recess advocate for your state. Go to the website of the American Association for the Child's Right to Play (ipausa.org) to find out how. IPA/USA is the country's largest group advocating for elementary-school recess. It offers a comprehensive packet—free—to anyone who asks.

Having won their respective battles, Lauren Kincaid and Rebecca Lamphere continue to work in their own ways to ensure that other children reap the benefits of recess. Lauren is on a mission to inform the parents of younger children entering local elementary schools of the importance of recess—to guard against backsliding. And Rebecca, who's become the parent liaison for IPA/USA, wrote a resolution, adopted by the Virginia State PTA/PTSA, stating that the PTA/PTSA supports at-least-once-daily recess of no less than fifteen minutes. She currently has a resolution on recess submitted to the National PTA. Both women have compiled literature offering information to those wishing to fight for recess and are available for advice and support. Their E-mail addresses appear in the Resources.

Professionals in the early childhood field have for years trumpeted the importance of educating the "whole"—thinking, feeling, moving—child. Yet more and more, we continue to behave as though children consist of heads only, which are separate from and unrelated to bodies and emotions. If we can't ensure this misguided attitude doesn't prevail in the classroom, we can at least make sure our children experience daily recess because that truly is a time when the whole child is addressed.

9

Preparing Your Child for a Lifetime of Physical Activity

"Never doubt that a small group of thoughtful committed citizens can change the world. Indeed, it is the only thing that ever has."
—Margaret Mead

In an article at parentsknow.com, writer Bonnie Rosenstock recommends that those looking for a letter of the alphabet with which to label the next generation consider *O* for *Generation Obese*. Unfortunately, it's an appropriate suggestion, as today's children are the most obese on record.

Conversely, it would also make sense to choose the letter *H*—for *Generation Hyper*—as children today are living such scheduled lives that a day planner makes a more useful birthday gift than does a skateboard or bicycle.

Sadly, both of these descriptors apply to today's youth. Children may be constantly on the go but not in such a way that they're warding off unwanted pounds. And, even if they're not overweight, we have to remember that thin children, too, can be unfit. If a child is overwhelmed because he never gets any downtime, the stress can take its toll. If he participates in too little vigorous physical activity, either due to lack of time or lack of inspiration, "fit" is probably not an accurate way to describe his physical condition. And that's going to be the case whether it's evident on the outside or not. When the time comes for him to exert physical energy, he'll likely find his muscles, heart, and lungs aren't up to the challenge.

So, under which category will your child belong—Generation O, Generation H, or possibly Generation O/H? Which profile is most applicable to your child? Does she sit in front of the television and/or computer for hours on end? Or is she functioning like a robot on overdrive? Are you under the misguided impression that either of these scenarios is "normal"?

Clearly, many of today's parents have come to think of these situations as normal, but neither of them is. Children were meant to play—to run and jump and tumble! Maybe it can't be like it was in the "good old days," but children should be able to attain a balance between the two extremes prevalent in our current culture—to have a physically active lifestyle *without* burning themselves out in the process.

How much influence can you have as a parent? Can you really, through your words and actions, have an impact, not just on your child's present level of physical activity but on his future levels as well?

Absolutely! After all, you influence your child in other important ways—for example, her present and future morals—all the time. You wouldn't hesitate to teach your child right from wrong because you're unsure as to whether or not it would make a difference. Similarly, you shouldn't let her shape her physical condition and her attitude toward it on her own.

Here's some of what the research has to say about parental influence on children's levels of physical activity:

- Two studies demonstrated that both parental encouragement and discouragement had an almost immediate effect on the physical activity levels of children twenty to forty-six months old.
- One study showed that children's levels of physical activity increased when parents prompted them to play outside instead of watching TV or playing video games.
- Another study discovered a correlation between parents' prompts to be active and preschoolers' levels of physical activity at home.
- A number of studies have determined that active children sensed more encouragement from their parents than did inactive children.
- Active children more often informed researchers that their parents expected them to be physically active.
- The activity levels of elementary-school children show a direct correlation with the activity levels of their parents.

Throughout much of this book we've discussed what you can do to ensure a healthier, more physically active—but sensible—life for your child. At the end of the last several chapters we've addressed the question "What's a parent to do?" This final chapter will be all about what a parent—you—can do.

We'll explore simple methods, like adding more walking to your family's lifestyle, to more challenging solutions, such as what you can do as a member of your community. We'll delve a bit deeper into your responsibility as a role model. We'll address an issue faced by many of today's parents: how to respond when your child insists on playing sports before she's developmentally ready. Last, we'll talk about balance: why it matters and how you can help your child achieve it.

Lead by Example

There's no doubt about it. If you want to prepare your child for a lifetime of physical activity, it has to start now, while your child is very young. And the most important thing you can do toward that goal is to lead the way by being a role model. As confirmed by research, your influence is considerable. Sometimes it will take the form of words, other times action. But in either case you've got to keep it positive!

For example, research has shown that parents' *inactivity* may exert more influence on their children's behavior than being active does. That is, if your child sees you sitting in front of the TV during all your free time—if he never sees you exercising or enjoying yourself as you do something physical—your actions (in this case inactions) will speak volumes. He'll simply follow suit. Even if you *tell* him how important it is to be physically active, he'll have no reason to believe you. (Similarly, children who watch their parents smoke while delivering a lecture on the dangers of tobacco won't receive the message their parents intended.)

A Penn State study demonstrated that children do indeed follow the example their parents set for them. Their research, conducted over two years, established that 79 percent of the girls who became overweight from ages five to seven, with or without a genetic predisposition to obesity, were from sedentary families.

On the other hand, an article in the *Australian Journal of Nutrition and Dietetics* reports that children with active mothers are twice as likely to be active as children with inactive mothers. Children with active fathers are three and a half times more likely to be active than children with inactive fathers. And when both parents are active, their children are *six times* more likely to be active!

According to additional research, although today's children aren't usually taught how to play and be physically active, they do "catch" the attitude of their parents and siblings toward play and sports. In other words, attitude is as contagious as the common cold. So, if you want your child to have a great attitude toward physical activity, you'll have to have one, too.

Here your words can play an important role. However, you should give careful consideration to what you do or don't say.

For instance, a series of studies conducted in the 1990s discovered that parents' enjoyment and encouragement of physical activity had a significant impact not only on their children's attitude toward physical activity but also on their feelings of competence in it. Unfortunately, parents gave more encouragement to their sons than to their daughters. As a result the girls perceived they had less physical competence, and they didn't feel as good about physical activity as did the boys.

Also, the words you choose when a child asks to go outside to play can foster either positive or negative feelings about play and movement. If you respond enthusiastically to the child's request, positive feelings will flow. If, however, you place constraints on your permission—"OK, but don't get dirty"; "OK, but play nice"; "OK, but stay on the porch"—you're giving the impression that you'd rather she just stay *still*.

Then there are your actions. If you want your child to move, you've got to get moving, too. Yes, time, in this day and age, is an issue. Often both parents are working. Children are enrolled in child-care settings from the time they're infants. And if your child is school-age, he's involved in any number of after-school activities.

Surprisingly, though, the research shows parents are spending *more* time with their children today than did parents in the recent past. A study conducted by the University of Michigan, which looked at two-parent families with children between the ages of three and twelve, discovered that, in 1997, children spent around thirty-one hours a week with their mothers and twenty-three hours a week with their fathers. This was up from twenty-five and nineteen hours, respectively, in 1981. According to the authors of the study, the results are due to a trend of greater parental involvement in child development.

However, a University of Minnesota study determined that today's children are spending 25 percent less time playing and 50 percent less time in unstructured outdoor activities. Obviously, then, the increase in "family time" isn't being spent playing—inside or out.

This doesn't have to be the case for your family, though.

You might find it difficult, at first, to set aside time for something you consider an "extra." But playing is so much more than that. Play is, according to Friedrich Froebel (known to early childhood educators as the "father of the kindergarten"), "the highest expression of human development in childhood." When you take the time to join in your child's play, you're helping to promote that development. You're also saying—so much more emphatically than you could with words—that play is a good thing.

Furthermore, playing together is the simplest way for the two of you to get some physical activity. And, unlike with efforts to get your child to eat her peas, you won't have to worry about getting resistance from her. Children were born to move; they take to play like birds to the sky. They also love having your company and your undivided attention. Your only "problem" may come when it's time to stop playing!

Of course, there are some rules you'll have to play by.

The main one? Remember that this is *your child's* play! When children play, they decide what they want to do, and they set the rules. More important, they don't have a *purpose* in mind. Play exists for its own sake. If you start imposing your plans and policies on a child, it's no longer play. But if you can remember what it's like to be a kid again—to go with the flow and to look at things through her eyes (a rock doesn't necessarily have to be a rock, and a toy can have many, often unusual uses), you'll be giving your child an invaluable gift that can easily last a lifetime. In brief, don't approach play as an adult!

However, to further serve as a role model as an adult, you can plan parties, outings, and vacations around physical activity. Looking for something to do on a Saturday afternoon? Go to the roller-skating rink. Planning a vacation? How about a trip to the mountains, where you can hike and swim, rather than to an amusement park, where you'll stand in lines and then sit on rides? Will you be inviting dozens of your child's friends to a backyard birthday party? Why not set up play stations—one with bubbles to chase, another with balloons to volley, and still another with beanbags to balance— where the children, divided into groups, play for a while and then rotate?

Additionally, as mentioned in Chapter 5, you should buy gifts related to physical activity, like roller skates, a croquet set, or hiking boots. If you give your child computer games and videos, you're giving him the wrong impression.

And, of course, don't forget house and yard work. If everyone in the family does it together, it's going to be a more enjoyable experience. Running the vacuum cleaner, dusting the furniture, washing the car, and raking the leaves are all activities that burn calories. Play a moderate- to fast-paced piece of music in the background, and you'll probably burn even more calories keeping time with the rhythm. Or family members could skip or march their way through chores. How about raking the leaves or washing the car while moving only in a backward direction? (Who says chores can't be fun?)

Finally, don't forget about the television. The best and simplest activity-promoting thing you can do is to turn it off! If your child doesn't yet have a TV set in her bedroom, don't put one there. If she already has one, take it out. And, to be the finest possible role model, you should remove the set from your bedroom, too. (Check out tvturnoff.org for more ideas.)

Walk the Walk

Making time for play and then actually doing it will bring you and your child immeasurable joy and benefit. But unless you play *really hard* several times a week, you and your child probably won't be getting enough exercise to benefit your health to the extent you should. So, you'll also need to make other forms of activity a regular part of your family's lifestyle. The simplest way to do that? By doing something we've been practicing since we were about twelve months old: walking.

People just don't walk much these days. Oh, they *walk*—to the car, from the car, into a building, to the escalator, and then maybe to the desk where they sit most of the day. But they don't walk to *go* somewhere or for the simple sake of walking.

As a form of exercise, walking is almost perfect. It's an exercise just about everyone can do, regardless of fitness level. It doesn't require special skill, and you can do it at your own pace. There are no fees involved, and there's no equipment required. Also, it can be both practical (it can get you where you need to go) and pleasurable (you can take in the sights and have a heart-to-heart with your child), while also burning calories.

Walking as a family can provide more quality time. For those with an overwhelming need to accomplish more than one thing at a time, it's the perfect activity for multitasking. If your family regularly takes a walk after dinner, on Saturday mornings, or after attending weekend services, you'll be guaranteeing both physical and emotional health. Surely there's no better use of your time than that. You can even take the family dog with you and serve three purposes at once.

Still, it's estimated that the average school-age child or office worker takes only three to five thousand steps a day. It's recommended that we take ten thousand steps a day. Doing so would burn an extra two thousand to thirty-five hundred calories a week. And if just a small percentage of individuals began doing so, the United States alone would see a savings of billions of dollars in health care related to heart disease.

Beyond immediate health concerns, however, there's the subject of this chapter: ensuring a *lifetime* of physical activity and good health for your child. If that's your goal (and, if you're reading this book, it probably is), you'll have to instill in your child the attitude that walking is a way of life.

Unfortunately, if she's typical of today's children, *being driven* is a way of life. And the only way her thinking is going to change is if yours does.

Is your child going to a friend's house a few blocks away? Stop yourself from getting in the car and walk him there instead. Going to the mall or grocery store? Don't circle the lot for endless minutes, searching for the spot closest to the door. Think about the message that sends and instead park—enthusiastically—far from the door and take a brisk little hike. Do you have a choice between taking the elevator and walking a couple flights of stairs? Choose the latter and whistle a happy tune on your way!

Of course the idea of scheduling walking into our lives may feel strange to those of us who didn't need to *plan* physical activity when we were children. Among other things, we walked long distances to school five days a week, thereby getting more than enough exercise to meet the current standards. Today, however, 85 percent of our children's trips to school are by car or bus. While it may no longer be practical for any variety of reasons to send our children out the door and on their merry way in the morning, you should know there are still ways to get them to school under their own steam.

Among the goals of Healthy People 2010 are to:

- Increase the proportion of children's trips to school less than or equal to one mile made by walking from 31 percent to 50 percent
- Increase the proportion of children's trips to school less than or equal to two miles made by bicycling from 2.4 percent to 5 percent

With this in mind, the Centers for Disease Control (CDC) has taken up the cause, with its KidsWalk-to-School program. The goals of the program are to:

- Increase opportunities for physical activity by encouraging children to walk and bike to school in groups accompanied by adults
- Encourage communities to build coalitions to create an environment that is supportive of safe walking and bicycling to school

Among the issues the program addresses are the importance of physically active travel, crime prevention, and, because today's communities are designed with vehicles in mind, pedestrian safety.

A number of states have already been inspired by the program, with twenty-nine of them passing legislation to create councils to promote physical activity. Taking it a step further are the states of California and South Carolina, the former of which, in 1999, allocated $20 million for two years to redesign roads to decrease traffic speed, install traffic control equipment, and improve sidewalks and bike paths. In 2000 the South Carolina Governor's Council on Physical Fitness presented twenty-eight schools with money to conduct a Walk Our Children to School Day.

To receive a copy of the KidsWalk-to-School guide, you can call 888-232-4674. To download it or obtain more information, go to cdc.gov. In addition, you can find information about:

- National Walk to School Day at walktoschool-usa.org
- International Walk to School Day at iwalktoschool.org
- Organizing a "walking school bus" at heartandstroke.ca.

It Takes a Village

Obviously there are just some things you can't do on your own. Creating a plan to walk the neighborhood kids to school is one of them. There are also plenty of other worthy projects for which you'll want to enlist the help of your neighbors and community. All it takes is one person who believes she can make a difference, and, before you know it, the power of that belief has others involved. And then watch what happens!

In Maine, Franklin County had higher rates of heart disease, diabetes, and high blood pressure than most of the rest of the state. Because the county's residents relied on their cars to get around and the most affordable restaurants served the fattiest food, obesity—and its resulting health problems—had become a real concern. But a group of dedicated medical professionals got together and decided things had to change.

They called themselves the Rural Health Associates, and their volunteers took a variety of actions. They tested shoppers' blood pressure and cholesterol at local grocery stores, offering personal nutrition advice while they were there. They persuaded schools to invite adults to exercise by walking their halls (an especially important victory, as harsh New England winters can keep even the heartiest of souls from exercising outdoors). And they convinced the local university to allow residents to use its gym.

Today Franklin County can be proud of having one of the lowest death rates of any Maine county. They also have the second lowest percentage of overweight and obese adults. But that doesn't mean they're finished! Now known as the Healthy Community Coalition, the original group, along with the help of hospital administrators, businesspeople, politicians, and about four hundred locals, plans and implements ideas for healthy living. One of them is Stride into Summer, a community walking program.

What can you do in your area? That depends on what your community and your child need.

At the simpler end of the spectrum may be your child's need for playmates. Do other children her age live too far away, or are those who live nearby all involved in organized activities and sports? If so, your first goal may be to form a play group. Talk to other parents at her school or childcare center. Let people know—in your neighborhood, at church, at the library—what you're trying to do. You may find other parents who'd also prefer a play group over organized sports but thought the latter was their child's only chance for socialization and physical activity.

Often play groups rotate from home to home. But if you'd also like someplace safe and spacious for the children to play, do as the residents of Franklin County did: convince the local university or school to open its gym to the public on nights and weekends. Perhaps the basement of a religious center would serve the purpose. Enlist the support of area pediatricians and others interested in seeing children physically active.

Is there a local playground? Sign up volunteers to take the play group there on a rotating basis so the children can have valuable outdoor time.

Finally, be sure to schedule your play group for both mornings and evenings so it's also available to parents—mothers *and* fathers—who work outside the home.

Once everything's organized, you can introduce the children to games and activities you've collected for them to play—indoors and out, in small and large spaces. Remain on the lookout for new ideas. Most important, don't just sit and have coffee while the children play. Join in the fun and make note of those games the two of you can play at home.

Another worthy cause for you to take on might be the local playground itself. How well maintained is it? Does it meet current safety standards? Are you concerned about children playing there without adult supervision? Here, too, you can recruit friends and neighbors to help you turn things around. After all, what good is a playground that remains empty? Or that could possibly be harmful to children?

With many streets and neighborhoods considered unsafe for children's play and with corner lots no longer empty and ball fields filled with organized sports, playgrounds take on even greater importance today than in the past. If you have one nearby, count your blessings and then do what you can to ensure it's a safe, happy place for your child. There are organizations concerned with playground safety that will provide you with the information you need and help you get started. (They're listed in the Resources.)

Want to help others in your community understand the value of play? Organize a PlayDay, an event intended to bring people together "to play for the sake of playing, to challenge each individual, and to share in the joy of discovery and interaction." So says the website of the American Association for the Child's Right to Play (ipausa.org/playdayorg.htm). The website provides everything you need to know to plan such a day, from choosing a location to involving other individuals and organizations to selecting appropriate games to play. Maybe you could plan a PlayDay during the month of May, which has been designated National Physical Fitness and Sports Month.

And what about opportunities for walking and biking in your community? Are there safe, well-maintained sidewalks and bicycle paths, or is driving the only possibility for getting around town?

Do the local schools offer both recess and physical education? Do the after-school programs include plenty of physical activity, or are the children sitting around, doing arts and crafts, playing board games, or doing more schoolwork?

These are among the questions you'll want to ask as you determine what battles you want—or need—to wage. But whatever you decide, you don't have to go it alone. Enlist your friends and fellow citizens to fight alongside you. And contact organizations, like those listed here and in the Resources, to provide support. That's what they're there for. Again, children value what's of value to the important adults in their lives. If your child witnesses the efforts made by her family members and neighbors on behalf of physical activity, those efforts will make an impression on her that will last a lifetime.

If Your Child Wants to Play Sports

"But, Mom [Dad], all the other kids are playing soccer [T-ball, hockey, football]. I wanna play, too!"

Does this sound familiar? Have you heard this refrain or something similar in your house? Maybe you've done everything right where physical activity is concerned: played with your child, arranged play groups for social contact and more movement opportunities, scheduled family hikes and walks and trips to the park, and so on, and so on. But still your little one insists on also playing sports.

Of course, based on what you've read in this book or what you may have read or learned elsewhere, you know participation in organized sports before the age of eight (or at least six) is far from ideal. It doesn't provide enough physical activity. It doesn't offer skill instruction or enough opportunity for skill improvement. It's often too competitive and therefore stressful for young children. And children under the age of eight don't possess the physical, cognitive, social, or emotional skills to participate successfully in organized sports. You're also aware, by now, that your child will not be left behind—in terms of skill development or preparation for sports participation—if he doesn't start as early as all the other kids do!

But he wants to play. It's an all-too-common scenario in today's culture. What's a parent to do?

Well, if you absolutely cannot talk her out of it, the most important thing you can do is make sure any experience your child has with sports is a positive one. Otherwise the possibility of a lifetime of physical activity is in real jeopardy. But just this one task entails quite a lot.

Since too often children are enrolled in sports that their *parents* are excited about, you'll first want to ask your child what sport he's interested in. Does he want to play a team sport, like hockey, or does he prefer an individual sport, like swimming? Choice, you may recall, is essential to both enjoyment and a sense of autonomy. And, regardless of the choice he makes, he'll want and need your full support—even when he changes his mind and decides he wants to try something else.

Also, bear in mind that any time you place a child in a situation for which she's not prepared, failure is the likely result. With failure comes loss of confidence and self-esteem and, ultimately, a feeling of worthlessness. Surely this isn't what you want for your child and should be avoided at all costs.

Children join sports programs because they want to have fun. Failure isn't fun, especially when you're too young to understand why you're failing; when, no matter how hard you try, you still can't succeed. While it isn't necessary to succeed all the time, a child will have fun if at least the potential for success is present. And that potential is most apt to exist when there's a balance between the child's skill level and the challenge of the activity. If the challenge is too easy, boredom sets in. If it's too difficult, learned helplessness is often the eventual result.

So, once your child has expressed interest in a particular sport, your first job will be to look for a program that doesn't treat children as small adults or, worse, small versions of professional athletes, which is harmful on any number of levels. In other words you don't want to enroll your child in a program where he's expected to play games (or, in a sport like swimming or karate, to take part in competitions) that haven't been modified radically for young children—where he's expected to use physical, social, emotional, and cognitive skills he hasn't yet acquired.

What do you look for instead? Look for a program where they actually teach children the skills they'll need to eventually play their chosen sport. Yes, some of the instruction can involve playing games. But these games shouldn't involve winning and losing. Nor should they be played in the traditional manner. Fields should be smaller, balls softer, equipment child-sized, and games shorter. Additionally, rules should be minimal, and there should be a small number of players per team.

Is your child having fun? Staying interested? Then it's the right choice for her. If the answer to either of these questions is no, it's time to look for something else.

To help you know what to look for, there are organizations dedicated to sports parenting listed in the Resources. Also, the National Alliance for Youth Sports has created a program called Start Smart that, according to their brochure, "prepares children for the world of organized sports without the threat of competition or the fear of getting hurt." With this program, parents and children work together to create a supportive environment in which children can learn the basic skills required of sports like softball, baseball, soccer, and more. You can call them at 800-729-2057, or look them up at nays.org.

Of course, once your child is settled into something he enjoys, there's still a lot for you to do. Most important, you'll have to demonstrate the appropriate attitude at all times. This means, first and foremost, that you must have realistic expectations for your child! Otherwise there's disappointment in store for everybody.

A young child wants more than anything to please you. If you place too much emphasis on her skill—or lack thereof—she won't be able to please you, no matter how hard she tries. If you offer her more criticism than praise—even when it's intended, out of love for her, to "help"—you can cause extreme anxiety. In some cases, if a child pushes too hard, injuries can result.

If success for you equals winning, the stress of losing can be overwhelming to a child. Winning is an adult goal. As such it's the adults who are overcome with emotion during game situations. It's the adults, more than the kids, who are unable to conduct themselves appropriately when children play. You've heard some of the stories. Following are a few that have made the news:

- The most recent incident, as this book is being written, is headlined "Spectator bites off man's ear during post-game brawl at youth baseball tournament." During the same incident, an infant girl was knocked from her mother's arms.

- A father uses a hockey stick to break the nose of his ten-year-old son's coach.

- A former police officer is convicted of soliciting assault after he offered $2 to a ten-year-old Little League pitcher to bean an opposing player.

- A gun is fired at a peewee football game.

- A mother attacks a fourteen-year-old referee.

According to the National Alliance for Youth Sports, the rate of violence among parents at youth athletic events has *tripled* since 1995. One of the unfortunate results of this bizarre behavior was evident in a survey of hundreds of eight- to eighteen-year-old children, who reported they think violence is an appropriate way to handle conflicts.

Another unfortunate result of the win-at-all-costs attitude, among both parents and coaches, is that the children themselves are being abused verbally and physically. A survey by the Minnesota Amateur Sports Commission determined that almost half of the children involved in sports said they'd been yelled at or insulted. As many as 17.5 percent reported they'd been hit, kicked, or slapped. And just over 8 percent confirmed they'd been coerced into harming someone else.

If your child chooses to be involved in sports, abuse is the last thing you would expect him to get from the experience! Nor do you want him to learn bad sportsmanship—spanning the range from pouting after a lousy game to using dirty tricks or violence on opposing players. To prevent the former, you must be diligent in your choice of a program. To prevent the latter, you must not only choose the right program but also—no matter what—display good sportsmanship yourself. As mentioned earlier in the chapter, children are more likely to do as you do than to do as you say.

Again, children choose to participate in sports because they want to have fun. So fun is what you need to emphasize with both your words and actions. Talk to your child after each time she takes part in her chosen program. Reinforce the positives and the successes—not in terms of wins but in terms of skills improved, display of a great attitude, friendships, and enjoyment. *Smile* as you watch your child play. And if a program stops being fun for either one of you, take a step back and ask why. Then make the necessary changes.

Don't forget, too, that sports participation—even the developmentally appropriate kind—is not going to provide enough physical activity. Think of it as supplemental to unstructured play and all the other movement your child experiences. And keep encouraging him to try new things, including new sports, because it's too soon to specialize. Research tells us that children who experience a variety of physical activities and wait until after puberty to specialize are the ones who most benefit in the long run. Not only do they suffer fewer injuries, but also they remain with their chosen activity longer than do those who specialize early.

Striking a Balance

Balance. It's a word that has perhaps become overused in today's society, as we adults endlessly converse about and contemplate achieving it in our lives. We strive for a balance between work and family, labor and leisure, obligation and recreation, the competition of the workplace and our need to connect with others. But while many are striving for balance, few are achieving it.

For a great many contemporary adults, *balance* is a word that has come to symbolize something out of reach. Something desired but elusive, as we work long hours, tend to families, and spend what little free time we have as *productively* as possible. What used to be considered leisure time (remember lazy Sunday afternoons?) must now be *filled*. It doesn't matter whether it's with "recreation," chores of one kind or another, or shuttling the children here and there, just so long as we can say we didn't waste it. "What did you do this weekend?" has become a question to be reckoned with on Monday mornings. It demands a smart answer, just as surely as did our eighth-grade algebra teacher.

If you're an adult who's been giving balance some consideration—who's tired of the treadmill—perhaps you find yourself looking back fondly on what now seems to be an idyllic childhood. Back to the days when time stretched endlessly before you. Back when there were few demands on that time. And, except for summers, weekends, and days when the darkness fell too early, there always seemed to be plenty of it.

How sad that today's children won't have those memories to cling to when they become harried adults. Because they're already harried. There are all kinds of demands on their time. And all they have to look forward to is more of the same.

Quiet moments of solitude? Activity initiated and directed by the child? A break from the relentless competition so prevalent in society? No chance. Children are expected to be every bit as productive and competitive as adults.

In *Respectful Educators—Capable Learners*, Cathy Nutbrown writes:

> There is a sense of urgency about childhood—of hastening progress, of accelerating development. Is this born out of wanting the best for children or from some belief or value base which says the state of childhood is worth less than the state of adulthood and so we must do all we can to reach the day when childhood is over?

Childhood is supposed to be a special time—a time like no other in a person's life. As simplistic as it may sound, it's the time to be a *child*. So, in this section of the final chapter of this book, we're going to explore alternatives to jam-packed schedules, lives that revolve around constant, adult-directed activity, and an overemphasis on competition.

What does this have to do with ensuring our children a lifetime of physical activity? Plenty, actually. Although this is a book about helping children get enough physical activity, it's also a book intended to prevent them from getting too much—especially too much of the wrong kind. Because too much of anything—even the good stuff—is still too much. And often the result of "too much" is burnout—even for children.

So, yes, if we want our children to become and stay healthy—to enjoy physical activity now and for the rest of their lives—we have to make sure they don't burn out. We have to do what we can to ensure they don't someday cringe at the idea of going for a walk, a jog, or a swim at the end of the day. We have to do what we can to make certain they hang on to that love of movement they were born with.

Toward this goal, we can first ensure our children get a respite from activities structured and led by adults.

Sally Jenkinson, in *The Genius of Play: Celebrating the Spirit of Childhood*, contends that if we structure our children's lives so there's no time for free play, the least we can expect from them is frustration, resentment, and anxiety. "A backlog of unresolved feelings will accumulate," she says.

Unstructured, or free, play is essential to children's overall development. During unstructured play they get the relief they need from pressure to perform to somebody else's—an adult's—standards. Here the events are initiated and directed by the child, and children learn values that *aren't* handed down from the grown-ups in their lives. They make their own decisions and learn to take responsibility for them. They learn lessons that will last a lifetime.

Unstructured play also offers children a much-needed break from competition. Yes, competition will play a role in free play among groups of children. But it will be competition of their own making, worth only whatever value the children themselves place on it. It will be competition at a level the children themselves can understand. It won't be imposed on or

Putting Family First

According to a study conducted by the Family Social Science Department of the University of Minnesota, over the last twenty years there's been a 33 percent decline in families who regularly eat dinner together. Research further shows a 28 percent decrease in the number of families taking vacations and a 100 percent decrease in household conversations!

Over the same period structured sports time has doubled. Passive, spectator time—the kind involved in *watching* sports—has risen from thirty minutes a week to over three hours a week. And that doesn't even include time spent watching sports—or anything else—on TV!

For all of these reasons a group of citizens in Wayzata, Minnesota, founded Putting Family First, a grassroots organization "where family life is an honored and celebrated priority. The democratic theory underlying this work is that families can only be a seedbed for current and future citizens if they achieve a balance between internal bonds and external activities."

According to their website, the need for such an organization stemmed from the difficulty individual parents have in prioritizing family life in "a culture that defines good parenting as providing more and doing more for one's children." They explicitly state that they're not an antisports movement. However, while they believe sports can provide positive experiences, they consider today's "preoccupation with competition has diminished the rewards of sports" while also diminishing the quality of family life for many.

The group's "desired future for families" is that:

- Families make family time and family activities a high priority in their decision making.
- Families set conscious limits on the scheduling of outside activities to honor the values they hold about family time.
- Families set limits on television, the Internet, and other electronic media if these are dominating family life inside the home.
- Families seek out ways to participate together in activities that build and serve their communities.
- Schools, faith communities, neighborhoods, and other groups provide families with resources to develop deeper bonds in a fragmenting world.

- Schools, faith communities, neighborhoods, and other groups offer regular intergenerational activities so that whole families can participate.
- Community activity groups of all kinds have explicit working policies that acknowledge, support, and respect families' decisions to make family time a priority.
- Employers have explicit working policies that honor families' time and energy needs.

For more information about this organization, including information on starting a Putting Family First movement in your community, see the website at family life1st.org.

---

demanded of them. And if it starts to get out of hand, the children will simply change the rules so everyone can continue to play and have fun.

In fact, free play will be more about cooperation as evidenced by the latter statement. As mentioned in Chapter 2, the research shows that, given a choice, young children prefer cooperative activities to competitive ones. And that's a good thing. While we may very well live in a competitive world, we also live in a world that requires a great deal of cooperation. After all, doesn't life require cooperation between spouses and among family members? Don't coworkers need to learn to collaborate? How about members of a community dedicated to the goal of making their area a better place to live? Or committee members working together toward the completion of a project?

Where will children learn to cooperate—to be part of a society—if all they ever experience is competition? Wayne K. Foster, writing in the journal *Education*, maintains that learning to achieve "harmony in interpersonal affairs and other prosocial behaviors" is globally neglected. He adds: "If a child is trained to be competitive, this may actually produce less cooperative behavior and reduce the child's desire to help others in need. A child may even prefer to beat another child than to receive a reward for cooperating."

Although it's learned behavior, competition has been so ingrained in children by the time they're in elementary school that they initially distrust

opportunities to cooperate. When cooperative musical chairs is first introduced, many kindergarten children will be nearly immobile, afraid to move
from the front of a chair, even though they've been assured no one will be
eliminated. It might be comical to witness if it didn't make such a sad statement about what they've learned in their short lives.

If children are to become skilled at cooperation and learn to strike a
balance against the many competitive situations they'll face, they must have
opportunities to work together in situations of their own making and in
cooperative games. (Several cooperative games are described in Chapter 3.)
The work of researcher Terry Orlick has demonstrated that young children
exposed to cooperative games are later more likely to engage in cooperative
behavior than children with no experience with these kinds of games.

Cooperative games have the additional benefit of relieving the fear of
failure that is so prevalent in competitive situations and other areas of children's lives. Fear of failure takes the fun away. And, once again, without fun
children have very little incentive to play.

While play and movement are, of course, the ultimate goals in our
quest for healthy lifestyles for our children, life was also meant to have varying rhythms. No living creature is meant to be in constant motion. As Ilse
Plattner writes in *Child Care Information Exchange*:

> In nature we do not find punctuality. Sometimes winter comes earlier, other
> times later. And nature takes its rest. Each animal has times of rest; plants do
> not grow incessantly. In the same manner human beings cannot perform all
> the time.

Plattner contends that part of our responsibility to children is giving them
time. Although what they do with that time should be up to them, in
another effort to strike a balance for our children a "no-electronics" policy
should be enforced. Options, then, include reading a book, taking a stroll
(as opposed to a walk intended to burn calories), and simply daydreaming.
As mentioned in the last chapter, the latter is essential to a child's creativity. While it may look as if the child is doing nothing at all, it's during these
quiet times that she has the chance to imagine—to play with ideas.

It's ironic that we're increasingly part of a world requiring problem
solving, yet, with our devotion to using time "productively," we're raising

children who can't help lacking problem-solving abilities. Quiet time can help children develop critical- and creative-thinking skills. It also gives them a chance to relax. The ability to relax is an essential skill to possess, especially in today's world. But children will never learn this skill unless they practice it.

Subsequently, in addition to all the other ways in which we serve as role models, we must also show our children that we value quiet time, so they'll value it as well. Finally, we must show them—beyond all doubt—that we love and value them, not for what they do but for who they are.

If we can strike these delicate balances—between doing and being, between competition and cooperation, between superkid and couch potato—we'll know we've done our best to ensure healthier lives for our children, now and in the future.

Appendix A

Active Start: A Statement of Physical Activity Guidelines for Children Birth to Five Years

In 2002, the National Association for Sport and Physical Education (NASPE) released its first-ever guidelines related to physical activity for children from birth to five years of age. Its position is that:

> All children birth to age five should engage in daily physical activity that promotes health-related fitness and movement skills.

The twenty-six-page document was developed by a task force consisting of experts in the fields of motor development, movement education, exercise physiology, and child development. It offers five guidelines for each of three age groups: infants, toddlers, and preschoolers. Also included is an introduction, an overview, the rationale behind each guideline, frequently asked questions (with answers), a glossary, a chart of common motor behaviors by age, references, and resources.

Reprinted from *Active Start*, with permission of NASPE (1900 Association Drive, Reston, VA 20191, USA), are the guidelines themselves.

Infant Guidelines

1. Infants should interact with parents and/or caregivers in daily physical activities that are dedicated to promoting the exploration of their environment.
2. Infants should be placed in safe settings that facilitate physical activity and do not restrict movement for prolonged periods of time.
3. Infants' physical activity should promote the development of movement skills.
4. Infants should have an environment that meets or exceeds recommended safety standards for performing large-muscle activities.
5. Individuals responsible for the well-being of infants should be aware of the importance of physical activity and facilitate the child's movement skills.

Toddler Guidelines

1. Toddlers should accumulate at least thirty minutes daily of structured physical activity.
2. Toddlers should engage in at least sixty minutes and up to several hours per day of daily, unstructured physical activity and should not be sedentary for more than sixty minutes at a time except when sleeping.
3. Toddlers should develop movement skills that are building blocks for more complex movement tasks.
4. Toddlers should have indoor and outdoor areas that meet or exceed recommended safety standards for performing large-muscle activities.
5. Individuals responsible for the well-being of toddlers should be aware of the importance of physical activity and facilitate the child's movement skills.

Preschooler Guidelines

1. Preschoolers should accumulate at least sixty minutes daily of structured physical activity.
2. Preschoolers should engage in at least sixty minutes and up to several hours of daily, unstructured physical activity and should not be sedentary for more than sixty minutes at a time except when sleeping.
3. Preschoolers should develop competence in movement skills that are building blocks for more complex movement tasks.
4. Preschoolers should have indoor and outdoor areas that meet or exceed recommended safety standards for performing large-muscle activities.
5. Individuals responsible for the well-being of preschoolers should be aware of the importance of physical activity and facilitate the child's movement skills.

Copies of the complete document are available for $10 to members of the American Alliance for Health, Physical Education, Recreation and Dance and for $13 to nonmembers. You may order by mail through AAHPERD Publications, P.O. Box 385, Oxon Hill, MD 20750; by calling 800-321-0789; or online at aahperd.org/naspe. The order stock number is 304-10254.

APPENDIX B

IPA Declaration of the Child's Right to Play

THE IPA DECLARATION of the Child's Right to Play was originally produced in November 1977 at the IPA Malta Consultation held in preparation for the International Year of the Child (1979). It was revised by the IPA International Council in Vienna, September 1982, and Barcelona, September 1989.

The IPA Declaration should be read in conjunction with Article 31 of the UN Convention on the Rights of the Child (adopted by the General Assembly of the United Nations, November 20, 1989), which states that the child has a right to leisure, play, and participation in cultural and artistic activities.

What Is Play?
- *Children* are the foundation of the world's future.
- *Children* have played at all times throughout history and in all cultures.
- *Play*, along with the basic needs of nutrition, health, shelter, and education, is vital to develop the potential of all children.
- *Play* is communication and expression, combining thought and action; it gives satisfaction and a feeling of achievement.

- *Play* is instinctive, voluntary, and spontaneous.
- *Play* helps children develop physically, mentally, emotionally, and socially.
- *Play* is a means of learning to live, not a mere passing of time.

Alarming Trends Affecting Childhood

IPA is deeply concerned by a number of alarming trends and their negative impact on children's development:

- Society's indifference to the importance of play
- Overemphasis on theoretical and academic studies in schools
- Increasing numbers of children living with inadequate provisions for survival and development
- Inadequate environmental planning, which results in a lack of basic amenities, inappropriate housing forms, and poor traffic management
- Increasing commercial exploitation of children and the deterioration of cultural traditions
- Lack of access for third-world women to basic training in child care and development
- Inadequate preparation of children to cope with life in a rapidly changing society
- Increasing segregation of children in the community
- The increasing numbers of working children and their unacceptable working conditions
- Constant exposure of children to war, violence, exploitation, and destruction
- Overemphasis on unhealthy competition and "winning at all costs" in children's sports

Proposals for Action

The following proposals are listed under the names of government departments that have a measure of responsibility for children.

Health

- Play is essential for the physical and mental health of the child.
- Establish programs for professionals and parents about the benefits of play from birth onward.
- Ensure basic conditions (nutrition, sanitation, clean water and air) that promote the healthy survival and development of all children.
- Incorporate play into community programs designed to maintain children's physical and mental health.
- Include play as an integral part of all children's environments, including hospitals and other institutional settings.

Education

- Play is part of education.
- Provide opportunities for initiative, interaction, creativity, and socialization through play in formal education systems.
- Include studies of the importance of play and the means of play provision in the training of all professionals and volunteers working with and for children.
- Strengthen play provision in primary schools to enhance learning and to maintain attendance and motivation.
- Reduce the incompatibilities among daily life, work, and education by involving schools and colleges and by using public buildings for community play programs.
- Ensure that working children have access to play and learning opportunities outside of the system of formal education.

Welfare

- Play is an essential part of family and community life.
- Ensure that play is accepted as an integral part of social development and social care.
- Promote measures that strengthen positive relationships between parents and children.

- Ensure that play is part of community-based services designed to integrate children with physical, mental, or emotional disabilities into the community.
- Provide safe play environments that protect children against abduction, sexual abuse, and physical violence.

Leisure

- Children need opportunities to play at leisure.
- Provide time, space, materials, natural settings, and programs with leaders where children may develop a sense of belonging, self-esteem, and enjoyment through play.
- Enable interaction between children and people of all backgrounds and ages in leisure settings.
- Encourage the conservation and use of traditional indigenous games.
- Stop the commercial exploitation of children's play and the production and sale of war toys and games of violence and destruction.
- Promote the use of cooperative games and fair play for children in sports.
- Provide all children, particularly those with special needs, with access to a diversity of play environments, toys, and play materials through community programs such as preschool play groups, toy libraries, and play buses.

Planning

- The needs of the child must have priority in the planning of human settlements.
- Ensure that children and young people can participate in making decisions that affect their surroundings and their access to them.
- When planning new or reorganizing existing developments, recognize the child's small size and limited range of activity.
- Disseminate existing knowledge about play facilities and play programs to planning professionals and politicians.
- Oppose the building of high-rise housing and provide opportunities to mitigate its detrimental effects on children and families.

- Enable children to move easily about the community by providing safe pedestrian access through urban neighborhoods, better traffic management, and improved public transportation.
- Increase awareness of the high vulnerability of children living in slum settlements, tenements, and derelict neighborhoods.
- Reserve adequate and appropriate space for play and recreation through statutory provision.

Affirmation

IPA is determined to sustain the momentum created by the International Year of the Child in 1979 to arouse world opinion for the improvement of the life of children and:

- **Affirms** its belief in the United Nations' Declaration of the Rights of the Child, which in Article 7 states, "The child shall have full opportunity to play and recreation, which should be directed to the same purposes as education; society and the public authorities shall endeavor to promote the enjoyment of this right"; and endorses its belief in Article 31 of the Convention on the Rights of the Child.

- **Recognizes** that the population of children in developing countries is three-quarters of the world's total child population and that efforts directed at the promotion of education and literacy and the stopping of environmental deprivation would improve the capacities of the poorest.

- **Affirms** its commitment to working with other national and international organizations to ensure basic conditions of survival for all children in order that they may fully develop as human beings.

- **Acknowledges** that each country is responsible for preparing its own courses of public and political action in the light of its culture, climate, and social, political, and economic structure.

- **Recognizes** that the full participation of the community is essential in planning and developing programs and services to meet the needs, wishes, and aspirations of children.

- **Assures** its cooperation with UN agencies and other international and national organizations involved with children.

- **Appeals** to all countries and organizations to take action to counteract the alarming trends that jeopardize children's healthy development and to give high priority to long-term programs designed to ensure for all time the **child's right to play**.

Organization

- IPA is an interdisciplinary nongovernmental organization, providing an international forum and advocacy for the promotion of play opportunities.
- IPA membership is open to any individual, group, or organization that endorses the IPA Declaration of the Child's Right to Play.
- IPA organizes regional and national conferences, workshops, symposia, and study tours and holds a triennial World Congress. IPA also publishes a magazine, *PlayRights*, and produces publications and audiovisual material on aspects of play.
- IPA offers advice to national governments and UN agencies on issues and problems related to the implementation of the Child's Right to Play.

IPA and the United Nations

In 1971 the IPA Board decided that it was important to cooperate with the UN organizations. We are recognized by ECOSOC (Economic and Social Council) and UNICEF and work in agreement with their principles. They give a context to our work, as follows:

1. Our focus on human rights, specifically the Child's Right to Play as stated in the UN Declaration of the Rights of the Child and now embodied in the Convention on the Rights of the Child.
2. Our feeling of solidarity with children all over the world.
3. Our involvement in peace education; IPA has been appointed as a Messenger of Peace by the United Nations.
4. Our commitment to the development of each individual to the maximum of his or her potential, the protection and enhancement of his or her culture, and the importance of the family and the community.

Appendix C

Choosing the Right Sport
or Physical Activity Program
for Your Child

In 1999 THE Youth Sport Coalition of the National Association for Sport and Physical Education (NASPE) created the following position statement. The purpose of the document is to help parents and guardians assess sport and physical activity programs prior to and after enrolling their children in them.

As you read through each of the following sections—Administration and Organization of the Program, Safety Considerations, Child's Readiness to Participate, Parent/Guardian Commitment to Child's Participation, and Evaluation of the Program—you should be able to assign an affirmative response to each statement. But please remember that this document was written with youths of all ages in mind and doesn't give special consideration to the under-eight set. Therefore, many of the statements apply specifically to organized sports, which this book does not recommend for children under eight. Also, statements such as "I am willing to adjust family time as necessary to support my child's participation," found under Parent/Guardian Commitment to Child's Participation, are—according to this book's philosophy—more appropriate for the parents of adolescents and teens. (But even the parents of adolescents and teens should maintain balance and family life as priorities!)

The following is reprinted with permission of the National Association for Sport and Physical Education, 1900 Association Drive, Reston, VA, 20191, USA:

There has been a proliferation of programs promoting sport and physical activity for children and youth. Due to diversity in program philosophies, objectives, facilities, and leadership, it is imperative that parents/guardians assess program quality, both initially and periodically, to determine if the program will be a positive experience for their child—physically, socially, and emotionally.

Participation in youth sports and physical activity programs can contribute positively to the development of:

- Physical fitness and a healthy lifestyle
- Self-confidence and self-esteem
- Motor skills
- Social skills
- Sportsmanship and ethics
- Fun and enjoyment of physical activity

The development of these important life skills should be central in a quality program. This checklist is designed to help parents assess program quality.

Consider each of the following statements as you evaluate school- or community-based physical activity programs for your child. Also consider the characteristics of your child (skill level, maturity, interests, special needs) in relation to each area and its components.

Administration and Organization of the Program

1. There are written policies for the program that include:
- Philosophy of program
- Selection of coaches and officials
- Training of coaches and officials
- Parental education and involvement

- Number and length of practices, contests, and tournaments appropriate for age group
- Selection of teams based on age, size, skill, and emotional development

2. The philosophy of the program includes:
- Adequate participation in practices and contests with no discrimination based on ability, gender, or race
- Development of fair play, teamwork, and sportsmanship
- Having fun
- Emphasis on winning with individual and team awards kept in proper perspective
- Communication with coaches, parents, officials, and participants
- Evaluation of coaches, officials, and program

3. Parental education includes:
- Requirements of the program, including costs, insurance coverage, practices, and contests
- Rules and regulations of the program and sport
- Proper conduct, showing respect for and support of the coaches and officials
- How to be a positive supporter

Safety Considerations

- Facilities are clean and hygienic
- Equipment and competition areas are safe and in good repair with regular inspection, maintenance, and replacement schedules in place
- Equipment is selected/adjusted based on the size and skill level of participants
- Practice and competition areas are free of obstacles and hazardous materials
- Necessary safety equipment is present (e.g., mats, protectors, body gear, spotting rigs)

- First aid supplies are on site and accessible at all times and are regularly inspected and replaced as used/needed
- Emergency medical forms, provisions, and personnel are available and easily accessible
- The ratio of coaches to staff (e.g., 1:10) to participants is appropriate for providing adequate instruction, supervision, and safety at all times for the age and skill level of the participants
- Warm-up and conditioning activities are part of the program to ensure safety and prevent injuries

Child's Readiness to Participate

- My child's interest level and desire to have fun match those of the group/team
- My child's skill level and size match those of the group/team
- My child's emotional and social maturity matches that of the group/team
- The level of intensity and competitiveness in the program matches my child's interest and ability
- Children with special needs are included in this group/team
- Cultural and gender diversity are encouraged through group/team structure, activities, and attitudes
- All children are treated with respect and given meaningful opportunities to learn skills and participate fully
- The challenges and expectations are appropriate for my child to develop a wide variety of fundamental skills prior to position specialization

Parent/Guardian Commitment to Child's Participation

- I will support my child's interests and realize that having fun is the most important reason children choose to participate in sport and physical activities

- I will provide the necessary time and assistance each week for my child to have a successful experience (e.g., encouragement, transportation, meeting attendance, volunteering, spectating)
- I understand the financial and time costs associated with participation and can provide for them
- I will respect and support decisions made by coaches and officials even though I may disagree with them, and I will discuss any concerns I have with the coach/staff in private
- I will be supportive of the coach/staff as teachers of my child
- I will provide insurance coverage for my child if the organization/league does not provide adequate coverage
- I will respect and follow rules and procedures of the club/league/organization providing the program for my child
- I am willing to adjust family time as necessary to support my child's participation
- I will support my child's active involvement by emphasizing participation, skill development, cooperation, and teamwork
- I will be a positive supporter who focuses on the positive aspects of youth sport and physical activity programs

Evaluation of the Program

- My child has fun
- My child's emotional and social maturity matches that of the group
- Team selection is appropriate
- The actual administration of the program is consistent with its stated philosophy
- Sufficient and appropriate equipment is available for all participants
- The number of practices, contests, and tournaments is appropriate to this level of activity
- Coaches modify activities to meet individual participants' needs
- Coaches/staff interact and communicate effectively with participants, parents, and officials
- Coaches treat participants, parents, and officials with dignity
- Coaches emphasize encouragement and positive feedback

- Coaches teach participants how to cope with negative feelings such as embarrassment, anger, frustration, and fear
- Coaches/officials are knowledgeable about the sport
- Coaches/officials demonstrate, teach, and encourage good sporting behavior
- Officials are fair and consistent in their rulings
- Awards are appropriate and emphasize participation, skill improvement, and teamwork

Resources

Physical Activity

Organizations offering policy statements or information concerning children and physical activity include the following:

- American Academy of Pediatrics: aap.org
- American Heart Association: americanheart.org
- Centers for Disease Control: cdc.gov/nccdphp/dnpa
- National Association for Sport and Physical Education: aahperd.org /naspe
- The Heart and Stroke Foundation of Canada: heartandstroke.ca

For articles on movement related to certain ages, go to medem.com and search on "movement and children" in their library.

To learn what you can do about physical activity at the community level, see *Promoting Physical Activity: A Guide for Community Action* by the U.S. Department of Health and Human Services. Champaign, Illinois: Human Kinetics, 1999.

Superkids

To read more about the issue of superkids in general, check out the following books:

- *Hyper-Parenting: Are You Hurting Your Child by Trying Too Hard?* by Alvin Rosenfeld, M.D., and Nicole Wise. New York: St. Martin's Press, 2000.
- *The Hurried Child* by David Elkind, Ph.D. Cambridge, Massachusetts: Perseus Publishing, 2001.
- *Keeping Your Kids Out Front Without Kicking Them from Behind: How to Nurture High-Achieving Athletes, Scholars, and Performing Artists* by Ian Tofler, M.D., and Theresa Foy DiGeronimo, M.Ed. San Francisco: Jossey-Bass, 2000.
- *Miseducation: Preschoolers at Risk* by David Elkind, Ph.D. New York: Alfred A. Knopf, 2000.
- *The Trouble with Perfect: How Parents Can Avoid the Overachievement Trap and Still Raise Successful Children* by Elisabeth Guthrie, M.D., and Kathy Matthews. New York: Broadway Books, 2002.

Children and Sports

There's plenty to read on this subject, including:

- *The Cheers and the Tears: A Healthy Alternative to the Dark Side of Youth Sports Today* by Shane Murphy, Ph.D. San Francisco: Jossey-Bass, 1999.
- *Just Let the Kids Play: How to Stop Other Adults from Ruining Your Child's Fun and Success in Youth Sports* by Bob Bigelow, Tom Moroney, and Linda Hall. Deerfield Beach, Florida: Health Communications, Inc., 2001.
- *Sports in the Lives of Children and Adolescents: Success on the Field and in Life* by Robert S. Griffin. Westport, Connecticut: Praeger, 1998.
- *Why Johnny Hates Sports: Why Organized Youth Sports Are Failing Our Children and What We Can Do About It* by Fred Engh. Garden City Park, New York: Avery Publishing Group, 1999.

- *Will You Still Love Me If I Don't Win?* by Christopher Andersonn. Dallas: Taylor Publishing Company, 2000.

And, of course, you can read a whole lot more about competition in Alfie Kohn's *No Contest: The Case Against Competition* (Boston: Houghton Mifflin, 1992). You might also want to check out Kohn's website: alfiekohn .org/parenting.

The following websites have information on sports parenting:

- sportsparenting.org
- nays.org (National Association for Youth Sports)
- MomsTeam.com
- positivecoach.com

Movement's Role in Learning

Books include:

- *Arts with the Brain in Mind* by Eric Jensen. Alexandria, Virginia: Association for Supervision and Curriculum Development (ASCD), 2001.
- *Learning with the Body in Mind: The Scientific Basis for Energizers, Movement, Play, Games, and Physical Education* by Eric Jensen. San Diego: The Brain Store, 2000.
- *Smart Moves: Why Learning Is Not All in Your Head* by Carla Hannaford. Alexandria, Virginia: Great Ocean Publishers, 1995.

Another resource, for use by parent volunteers in collaboration with elementary-school teachers, is Motor Moms and Dads: Physical Activities That Enhance Academic Success. Developed by Nancy Sornson, special education teacher consultant at Miller Early Childhood Center in Brighton, Michigan, the program offers a training video and accompanying manual. For more information, call Nancy Sornson at 810-229-0148, or E-mail her at nsornson@bas.k12.mi.us.

For a wonderfully accessible introduction to Howard Gardner's theory of multiple intelligences, read Thomas Armstrong's *Seven Kinds of Smart*

(New York: Penguin Books, 1993). Also, for a basic overview of MI theory—one that gets right to the heart of the issue for parents—you can go
to http://surfaquarium.com/mi.htm.

Fitness

To learn more about children's fitness, you might choose to read one or more
of the following:

- *50 Simple Things You Can Do to Raise a Child Who Is Physically Fit* by
  Joanne Landy and Keith Burridge. New York: Macmillan, 1997.
- *Fit Kids!: The Complete Shape-Up Program from Birth Through High
  School* by Kenneth H. Cooper, M.D. Nashville, Tennessee: Broad-
  man & Holman, 1999.
- *Your Child's Fitness: Practical Advice for Parents* by Susan Kalish.
  Champaign, Illinois: Human Kinetics, 1995.

You'll find plenty of family fitness ideas, including "Heart Smart
Quickies," at the website of the Heart and Stroke Foundation of Canada:
heartandstroke.ca. The Centers for Disease Control and Prevention also has
much to offer parents. Check out their site at cdc.gov/nccdphp/dnpa. To
download *Kids in Action*, a booklet of activity ideas for parents to do with
their children, go to fitness.gov/funfit.action.htm. You can also order a copy
of the booklet from the President's Council on Physical Fitness and Sports,
200 Independence Ave. SW, Room 738-H, Washington, DC 20201.

Physical Education

For information on physical education, the websites for these organizations
are helpful:

- National Association for Sport and Physical Education: aahperd.org
  /naspe
- PE Central: pecentral.org

- P.E.4Life: pe4life.org
- PELinks4U: pelinks4u.org

For comprehensive information on developmentally appropriate early childhood physical education, read *Experiences in Movement: Birth to Age Eight*, 3rd ed., by Rae Pica (Albany, New York: Delmar, 2004).

Recess and Outdoor Play

Books include:

- *Elementary School Recess: Selected Readings, Games, and Activities for Teachers and Parents*, edited by Rhonda L. Clements, Ed.D. Boston: American Press, 2000.
- *The Great Outdoors: Restoring Children's Right to Play Outside* by Mary S. Rivkin. Washington, D.C.: National Association for the Education of Young Children, 1995.
- *The Outside Play and Learning Book: Activities for Young Children* by Karen Miller. Beltsville, Maryland: Gryphon House, 1989.

Organizations and individuals offering information and support include:

- The American Association for the Child's Right to Play (IPA/USA): ipausa.org
- Do Children Need Recess?: geocities.com/recessplease
- National Association of Early Childhood Specialists in State Departments of Education: http://ericps.ed.uiuc.edu/naecs/position/recess play.html
- National Association for Sport and Physical Education (NASPE): aahperd.org/naspe
- Peaceful Playgrounds: peacefulplaygrounds.com
- Playing for Keeps: playingforkeeps.org
- Lauren Kincaid: kincaid3@cox.net
- Rebecca Lamphere: RecessMomVA@aol.com
- Deanna Ryan: deannamryan@yahoo.com

Playground Safety

- National Program for Playground Safety: PlaygroundSupervision.org
- National Recreation and Park Association: activeparks.org
- International Play Equipment Manufacturers Association: ipema.org
- U.S. Consumer Product Safety Commission: cpsc.gov

Games to Play with Babies

Here are three books that are chock-full of both activities and valuable information:

- *Creative Resources for Infants and Toddlers* by Judy Herr and Terri Swim. Albany, New York: Delmar Publishers, 1999.
- *Games to Play with Babies*, 3rd ed., by Jackie Silberg. Beltsville, Maryland: Gryphon House, 2001.
- *Your Child at Play: Birth to One Year*, 2nd ed., by Marilyn Segal, Ph.D. New York: Newmarket Press.

Activities for Children Eighteen Months to Eight Years

For lots of activity ideas, refer to the following:

- *Fundamental Motor Skills & Movement Activities for Young Children* by Joanne M. Landy and Keith R. Burridge. West Nyack, New York: The Center for Applied Research in Education, 1999.
- *Movement Activities for Early Childhood* by Carol Totsky Hammett. Champaign, Illinois: Human Kinetics, 1992.
- *Moving & Learning Series: Toddlers* by Rae Pica, with original music by Richard Gardzina. Albany, New York: Delmar, 2000.
- *Moving & Learning Series: Preschoolers & Kindergartners* by Rae Pica, with original music by Richard Gardzina. Albany, New York: Delmar, 2000.

- *Moving & Learning Series: Early Elementary Children* by Rae Pica, with original music by Richard Gardzina. Albany, New York: Delmar, 2000.

For more games and activity ideas, go to gameskidsplay.net.

Cooperative Activities

All the cooperative games you could ever want to play can be found in the following books:

- *Everybody Wins!: 150 Non-Competitive Games for Kids* by Cynthia MacGregor. Avon, Massachusetts: Adams Media Corp., 1998.
- *Everybody Wins: Non-Competitive Party Games and Activities for Children* by Judy Blosser and Gaylyn Larned. New York: Sterling Publishing, 1997.
- *Everybody Wins: 393 Non-Competitive Games for Young Children* by Jeffrey Sobel. New York: Walker & Company, 1984.
- *Everyone Wins!: Cooperative Games and Activities* by Sambhava and Josette Luvmour. Philadelphia: New Society Publishers, 1990.
- *The Second Cooperative Sports & Games Book: Over 200 Noncompetitive Games for Kids and Adults Both* by Terry Orlick. New York: Pantheon Books, 1982.

Another wonderful source of cooperative games is Family Pastimes. You can learn more about this company at familypastimes.com.

Miscellaneous

Other books you may want to explore include:

- *The Child and the Machine: How Computers Put Our Children's Education at Risk* by Alison Armstrong and Charles Casement. Beltsville, Maryland: Robins Lane Press, 2000.

- *Make-Believe: Games and Activities for Imaginative Play* by Dorothy
  Singer, Ed.D. and Jerome Singer, Ph.D. Washington, D.C.: Magina-
  tion Press, 2000.

For free and nearly free resources, including "Brain Facts," *Your Healthy
Baby*, and *The First Years Last Forever*, go to iamyourchild.org.

For information on early childhood, including the value of play and
choosing a preschool program, visit the website of the National Association
for the Education of Young Children: naeyc.org.

Index